WHISPERING LEAVES IN GROSVENOR SQUARE

Yuki Yoshida as a young woman.

Whispering Leaves in Grosvenor Square 1936-37

Yuki Yoshida

With

A FOREWORD BY H.E.HIROAKI FUJII
AMBASSADOR TO THE COURT OF ST JAMES

○

PEN-PORTRAIT OF YUKI YOSHIDA BY DOROTHY BRITTON

○

HISTORICAL SETTING BY IAN NISH

GLOBAL ORIENTAL

WHISPERING LEAVES
IN GROSVENOR SQUARE 1936-37
WITH A FOREWORD BY H.E. HIROAKI FUJII
PEN PORTRAIT BY DOROTHY BRITTON
HISTORICAL SETTING BY IAN NISH

By Yuki Yoshida

First published 1938 by
Longmans, Green and Co.

This edition first published 1997 by
GLOBAL ORIENTAL
PO Box 219
Folkestone, Kent CT20 3LZ
England

Global Oriental is an imprint of Global Books Ltd

© 1997 Global Books Ltd

ISBN 1-901903-00-1

British Library Cataloguing in Publication Data
A CIP catalogue entry for this book is available
from the British Library

Set in Bembo 13 on 15pt by Bookman, Slough
Printed & bound in England by Bookcraft, Midsomer Norton, Avon

Contents

Foreword

By H.E. Hiroaki Fujii
Ambassador of Japan to the Court of St James's

*W*hispering Leaves in Grosvenor Square is a moving piece of writing. When I read it, I was immediately struck by Madame Yoshida's delicate appreciation of nature and of her love of Britain. Her descriptions of the people she met and the events she witnessed testify to a profound sensitivity. At the same time, one cannot fail to note a sense of sadness, stemming from the deterioration in the friendship between the United Kingdom and Japan which she witnessed. The darkest days of our relationship were indeed beginning to unfold at that time.

However, despite the increasingly strident expressions of mutual antipathy heard in both Britain and

Japan in the mid-1930s, Madame Yoshida was encouraged by the unwavering friendship and support she received from her close acquaintances in this country. Her attachment to Britain and her treasured friendships with British people helped her through an otherwise trying period in her life.

Madame Yoshida epitomized what is best in modern Japan's tradition, as did her family. Her father, Count Nobuaki Makino, her grandfather, Toshimichi Okubo, and her husband, Shigeru Yoshida, were energetic promoters and supporters of an enlightened international role for Japan. Indeed, her grandfather had been a member of the Iwakura Mission, which visited the United Kingdom and other Western countries seeking inspiration for Japan's modernization, and whose 125th anniversary we celebrate this year.

Ambassador and Madame Yoshida remained devoted to promoting Anglo-Japanese relations when they returned to Japan. Their children also contributed to this ideal, in their different ways. In particular their daughter, Mrs Kazuko Aso, worked tirelessly in the furtherance of good relations between the two countries. She attended school in England during her parents' tour of duty in London, and later helped to found the Elizabeth-Kai, the ladies' equivalent of the Japan-British Society in Tokyo. Mrs Aso played a prominent role in her father's political career, following the death of her mother, and she accompanied her father, as his official hostess, during his time as Foreign Minister and later Prime Minister. She was thus in a unique position to understand the special nature of the relationship between the United Kingdom and Japan. The great esteem in which members of the Yoshida family were held was very evident at the memorial service for Kazuko Aso last year which my wife and I attended together with many of the Yoshida's British friends at the Church of the Immaculate Conception in Farm Street, just off Grosvenor Square.

Since Japan embarked upon the process of modernization last century, and especially following the Iwakura Mission, cordial relations between our two countries have been the norm. The period from the mid-1930s until the end of World War II was, therefore, a relatively short-lived, though nonetheless terrible aberration. It is to their great credit that Madame Yoshida and her family did what they could to perpetuate cordial relations between our two countries despite the discouraging circumstances that surrounded them. I know that the Yoshidas would be overjoyed to see how our friendship has flourished since the end of the war, particularly in the last decade or so. *Whispering Leaves in Grosvenor Square* is a work of great charm. For its author they may have been autumn leaves, whose ephemeral beauty presages the onset of winter. For me, however, they evoke spring and the approach of glorious summer. Anglo-Japanese relations are becoming steadily warmer and more fruitful, and everyone who reads this book will be pleased that Madame Yoshida's dearest wish has been fulfilled, although she herself was unable to witness this triumph.

Preface to the First Edition

By Sir Francis Lindley
Chairman of the Japan Society of London, 1936-42

M any in England may wonder in these days how it is that most of their fellow-countrymen who have lived in Japan feel a deep affection for that country and its people. This little memoir, written not in a spirit of propaganda but as a tribute of love to our country, will go far to explain.

The writer should need no introduction from me. The daughter of Count Makino was brought up in that atmosphere of wide and kindly culture unhappily more common everywhere before 1914 than since. No-where was it better represented than in Japan; and one cannot but wonder how many English people would enjoy playing what is described as the 'national game' of cards with poems written out on them. A kind of beggar-my-neighbour *in excelsis*. And what foreigner ever paid a more graceful tribute to our smoky capital than did Count Makino when he told his daughter that: 'London is like some priceless pearls wrapped in silk and stowed away in a bag. You cannot perceive its glory all at once but the longer you stay then the more you will be able to appreciate it.' With such an introduction from the father, no wonder London became dear to the daughter.

Appreciation of the beauties both of nature and of art is the heritage of the whole Japanese people – perhaps their most precious heritage. Madame Yoshida shares it to the full and gives expression to it more frankly and tenderly than is usual in our language. And the discerning reader will find rare gems woven into the main fabric of the tale – gems which proclaim the lady of quality, the statesman's daughter and the Ambassador's wife.

                                                                    F.O.L.

June 6th, 1938

Acknowledgements

The publishers wish to extend their sincere thanks to the following people whose interest, support and cooperation have been essential in returning this remarkable 'mini memoir' to print. In the first place, to both Dorothy Britton (Lady Bouchier) and Martyn Naylor of the Japan-British Society, Tokyo, who drew our attention to the very well received 1996 Japanese translation of the memoir by Shozo Nagaoka [*George Rokusei Taikanshiki to Chichibu no miya – Gurovune Sukuea no konoha no sasayaki* – published by Shin-Jimbutsu-Oraisha, Tokyo] and urged the desirability of reprinting the original English edition of Madame Yoshida's memoirs of London.

In turn, Dorothy Britton and Ian Nish (Professor Emeritus, London School of Economics) agreed to provide a pen-portrait of Yukiko Yoshida and an introduction to the historical backdrop of Anglo-Japanese relations in the late 1930s respectively, thus helping to illuminate both the person and the period in question for the benefit of readers at the end of the twentieth century.

We are most grateful to His Excellency Ambassador Hiroaki Fujii for kindly agreeing to provide a new (and most apt) Foreword to the new edition, to the Great Britain Sasakawa Foundation for their contribution towards the publication costs, as well as to Mr Taro Aso and Mr Masao Yoshida for giving us permission to reproduce a number of photographs from the family's private collection. In addition, we would like to acknowledge the kind assistance given by Sadaaki Nimata, Ikuno Fujii and the Japan Society of London.

Dorothy Britton also acted in part as 'picture researcher', as did Mr Nagaoka to help make the illustrations used in the book a valuable pictorial account of the Yoshida family in the pre-war years in general and Madame Yoshida's London period in particular; for their additional contribution to the project, we wish to extend our further thanks.

PUBLISHERS' NOTE
Madame Yoshida published her memoir under the name Yuki Yoshida. She was known simply as Yuki (snow) amongst her foreign friends. She was, however, Yukiko to her family and close Japanese friends, using the traditional *ko* suffixed to a girl's given name. *Ko* means 'child', and like our own archaic 'childe' was formerly used only by the nobility. Although used generally now, more and more Japanese women stylistically prefer to drop it, or use alternatives such as *e*. In the several contributions to this new edition she is referred to by both forms, as well as Madame Yoshida, which we have left as given out of respect for the contributor's wishes.

On the question of names, the Western convention of putting given names first has been used throughout, except in *Historical Setting* where the Japanese convention of putting family name first is applied (e.g. Yoshida Shigeru).

We have reproduced the text of *Whispering Leaves in Grosvenor Square* exactly as it appeared in the first edition.

THE YOSHIDA FAMILY

Marriage of Shigeru Yoshida & Yukiko Makino – March 1909

Shigeru Yoshida	born 22 September 1878
	died 20 October 1967
Yukiko Yoshida	born 9 May 1889
	died 7 October 1941
Sakurako Yoshida, daughter	born 1 June 1910
	died 29 January 1997
Kenichi Yoshida, son	born 27 March 1912
	died 3 August 1977
Koko Yoshida, daughter	born 15 January 1914
	died 19 July 1915
Kazuko Yoshida, daughter	born 13 May 1915
	died 15 March 1996
Masao Yoshida, son	born 10 August 1917

List of Illustrations

Yuki Makino (later Madame Yoshida) as a young girl, in formal young girl's *furisode*; possibly an o-miai photograph for showing to prospective bridegrooms.

Yuki Yoshida – A Pen-portrait

By Dorothy Britton
[Lady Bouchier]

H earing she was both artist and poet, I used to
wonder what Madame Yoshida was like as I
looked across at their house on the opposite corner of
Grosvenor Square from the club where I was staying in
1936 with my mother. Recently widowed, my mother
had brought me to England from Japan to go to
boarding school. Among our oldest and dearest
Japanese friends were the Okubos, and Mr Toshikata
Okubo, formerly London manager of the Yokohama
Specie Bank and later its president, was Madame
Yoshida's uncle (although only eleven years older than
she!). He had given my mother a letter of introduction

to the Japanese Ambassador and his wife. But alas, I was
not included when my mother was invited over there
for lunch, and to my further disappointment, Mr
Yoshida later came to lunch with us alone, Madame
Yoshida having been taken ill. I remember what good
company he was, and how amusing. The man who
would become Japan's first post-war prime minister
even then had Churchillian panache – complete with
hat and cigar.

It was not until I returned to Japan in 1949 that I
became good friends with two of the Yoshida children.
Their Cambridge-educated eldest son, Kenichi, a
brilliant essayist in both Japanese and English, produced
for a while in the fifties an attractive monthly magazine
about England, in Japanese, entitled *Albion*, to which I
often contributed, and in the early sixties we were both
members for several years of a panel of contributors to a
daily column in the *Asahi Shimbun*, Japan's leading
newspaper. On meeting Kenichi's wife I remember
how startled she looked when she heard my name.
Kenichi apologized, explaining that it was also the
name of their daughter Akiko's doll! I still feel
honoured to think a doll named 'Doroshii Buriton'
was part of that illustrious family. In 1959, Kenichi's
sister Kazuko, by then Mrs Aso, and I together founded
the Elizabeth Kai, the women's association of the
Japan-British Society.

The Yoshidas were a family of anglophiles. The
children were sent to English schools wherever their
father was posted, and consequently learned to speak
fluent English, which their mother always made a

point of speaking to them at home. They had a Japanese governess to see that they did not forget their mother tongue. Moreover, Mr Yoshida brought up his daughters, as well as his sons, in the English tradition of taking part in mealtime conversation and expressing opinions freely. In fact, they were scolded if, when asked their opinion, they had none. But it was a habit that later caused Kazuko to be severely chided by her husband as shockingly unladylike in a Japanese woman.

Nevertheless, Kazuko, who had been voted 'Miss Nippon' at fifteen and was the apple of her father's eye, had a glittering career all through his political life as his official hostess and companion after her mother's early death. With her fluent English, and sparkling personality, she graced the international scene with typical Yoshida flair, and became an honorary Dame Commander of the British Empire in 1975.

Judging by her photographs, Yuki Yoshida was a strikingly handsome woman, tall, with large dark eyes, a nobly sculptured nose, and sensuous lips. Her beauty and elegance were often spoken of in Western diplomatic circles. But according to Kazuko, that was because it was a European type of beauty. Yuki's mother, Countess Makino, one of the famous three lovely daughters of Viscount Mishima, was, on the other hand, stunningly beautiful, but in a somewhat more Japanese way, although from photographs I have seen her profile could have graced any European cameo. She was apparently aware of her good looks and given, unfortunately, to saying to her daughter:

'When I'm so beautiful, how could I have given birth to the likes of you?'

Naturally, this did little for Yuki's ego. Kazuko writes that she always thought of her mother as pretty, and was surprised when her mother once said: 'Since I'm so ugly, I've been studying myself in the mirror to see how much worse I can look!' Then, all of a sudden, she seemed to turn her eyes inside out, and her mouth inside out, too, and made a most extraordinary face, which Kazuko found quite alarming.

Yuki obviously had an unexpectedly humorous side as well as a serious one, although the serious aspect usually predominated. Her cousin Yuri Yasuda describes her as very reserved, with a gentle, slow manner of speech, totally unselfish, and generous in the extreme. She was frugal, hardly ever indulged herself, and if she possessed something she liked, she invariably wanted to give it away.

Her youngest son, Masao, remembers her self-disparaging modesty and her genuine conviction that she was totally undeserving of any praise, let alone happiness, even stoically accepting excruciating pain as a just reward for what she considered a worthless life.

She must have had no inkling of the inspiration she imparted to her family and friends. Masao, who went on to have a distinguished career in engineering, speaks glowingly of the way his deeply religious mother taught him to appreciate the beauty of nature as God's handiwork. She also instilled in him a love of music, encouraging his study of the violin. She herself played the violin, having studied it in Vienna as a girl, as well as singing.

Yuki was the daughter of the celebrated Meiji era politician and diplomat Count Shinken Makino (1861–1949). Although Nobuaki (sometimes read Shinken) was adopted by the childless Makino family, probably friends of his parents, he had been born the second son of statesman Toshimichi Okubo, one of the leaders of the Meiji Restoration that ended the long feudal period of military rule in 1868. Six years before his tragic assassination in 1877, Okubo travelled to Europe and America as part of the Iwakura Mission, taking with him his two elder sons whom he left behind at school in America for three years 'so they would grow up to become useful citizens of the new Japan'.

Nobuaki was then only ten years old. He eventually entered the foreign service and served in a variety of posts, including Minister to Italy and later Austria. Yuki was born in Rome, and spent much of her girlhood in Vienna; so when she married young Shigeru Yoshida, diplomatic life was not new to her. Their first posting together was to London. After a while they were transferred to Rome, where she had been born, and where she in turn gave birth to her first child, a daughter, whom they called Sakura (cherry blossom) an inspired pun on the name of the street, Via Sacra, where they lived.

Yuki then went on deliberately and conscientiously to make herself into a first-rate diplomatic wife. She applied herself to it as she would have to any of her artistic compositions. Having learned to speak German in Vienna, she set herself to perfecting her English – originally acquired at a convent school in Japan – constantly taking lessons in order to improve her pronunciation. She mastered the art of conversation and graceful social intercourse, in spite of the fact that she was not a party person by nature, preferring more quiet contemplative pursuits.

Before she accompanied her husband to England for the second time in 1920, her father, Count Makino, had likened London to a priceless pearl whose true worth would take time truly to appreciate. Simply hearing those words, she used to say, made her like England straight away!

She had studied poetry – particularly the composition of tanka – with the eminent Nobutsuna Sasaki, and her complete works were published posthumously in Tokyo in 1952. Over a hundred of the poems in that 5-line 31-syllable form were composed while in England, and she has included a number of them, romanized, with her own charming English translations, in this memoir. In fact, all of her prose reads like poetry, and her son Masao assures me that it is actually based on the rest of the tanka, poetically describing her day-to-day impressions of those eventful times, in flawless English. Her acute observations are combined with a typically Japanese sensitivity and aesthetic appreciation of the infinitely various aspects of nature.

Yuki's friends in England had urged her to publish her verses in English, and this book was the result. The publication of the original slim volume in 1938, bound in her favourite colour silver, was prompted by her longing to build a bridge of understanding between the two countries she loved so dearly, for Yuki was pained by the gradual worsening of Anglo-Japanese relations.

With her highly developed artistic sense, Yuki used to design the dresses made for her by her London couturier. She also designed patterns for decorating kimonos, and held several exhibitions at Takashimaya, one of Tokyo's elite department stores. Her designs were colourful, and original, appealing more to the younger generation than to older, conservative women. Yuki was masterful at contrasting colours. Essayist Kyoichi Usui who, as a youth, was taken to one of the exhibitions by his mother, still vividly remembers a striking kimono pattern that took his eye. It depicted Nikko's vermillion lacquer bridge crossing a ravine of luxuriant foliage. An Okubo cousin who owned one as a young girl described it lovingly to me: chrysanthemums of every description ran riot on a light green ground, while dark green leaves filled the hem, and a glimpse of chequerboard motif in gold and silver at the shoulder suggested the marquee of an Imperial chrysanthemum-viewing garden party. She told me it was a long-sleeved *furisode* that Madame Yoshida had specially designed with her in mind.

Yuki Yoshida adored flowers and called them her only extravagance. She never failed to dress stylishly but rarely bought more clothes than she needed. So much so that after her operation for cancer in the spring of 1941, she suddenly went on a most uncharacteristic kimono-buying spree, to her daughter's amazement, explaining that she did not want her

family to be embarrassed by a lack of the customary
posthumous mementos for handing out to relatives and
friends.

Yuki Yoshida died that October, just two months
before the outbreak of the Pacific War. The wife of the
American ambassador Joseph Grew, who was a
devoted friend, visited her daily in hospital and brought
delicacies that were becoming scarce, although Yuki,
unselfish to the end, protested that it was a waste to
bring them to one who had not long to live, and
begged her to bestow them elsewhere.

She was only fifty-one. Her last words were: 'I've
had a good life, a happy life.' But her daughter writes
that she wondered how her mother could have been
truly happy when she and her husband were so
incompatible – she so sensitive, artistic and highly-
strung, and he so self-assured and down-to-earth.

There was little warmth in their marriage, but they
had a deep respect for one another. Shigeru Yoshida
was famous for calling people *bakayaro* ('You fool!') on
the slightest provocation, but he was genial and very
likeable, and never failed to say 'thank you' and express
appreciation. Servants and geisha adored him.
Shun'ichi Kase (later Ambassador to the United
Nations) who served under him in London asked
him once why he always spoke to his wife in English
on the telephone. Yoshida replied: 'Because if we
speak in Japanese we invariably start quarrelling, but
my English isn't good enough for quarrels!' The
nervousness that went with Yuki's artistic temperament
irritated him. However, deep down he admired and

respected his wife's talents and her purity and innocence. With her sheltered upbringing, she was totally unworldly, which appealed to him. 'Your mother is an angel', he would often declare to his daughter – though never to his wife, alas. He was utterly heartbroken when she died. He summoned Mr Kase poste-haste from the Foreign Office to his home where Shun'ichi Kase found his mentor, a man who hated emotional display, trying desperately to smother his tears with a handkerchief. 'Be sure you take good care of your wife' he told his subordinate with feeling.

Sirens announced the start of the war in December, 1941. As the news crackled over the wireless, Count Makino muttered despairingly: 'To think it has come to this, after all my efforts for Japan!' The war years must have been a heartrending time for anglophiles like the Makinos and Yoshidas, who had done their best to avert hostilities. After his years as the first post-war prime minister, Yoshida wrote in his retirement: 'I opposed Japan's participation in World War II, but the only result was to attract the attention of our military police.' Though treated fairly decently, he subsequently spent a fortnight in a Kempeitai gaol.

It was perhaps just as well that the highly sensitive Yuki did not live to experience the sad interlude of the war.

BIBLIOGRAPHY

Essay 'The Art of Diplomacy' by Shigeru Yoshida. *This Is Japan*, Vol. 10, 1963.

Preface by Shun'ichi Kase to *Joji 6sei taikanshiki to Chichibu no miya: Gurovuna Sukuea no konoha no sasayaki* ('George VI's Coronation and Prince Chichibu: Whispering Leaves in Grosvenor Square') Japanese translation by Shozo Nagaoka, Shinjinbutsu Oraisha, 1996.

Yoshida fuufu no omoide (Memories of the Yoshidas) by Kyoichi Usui, postscript to the above.

Chichi, Yoshida Shigeru ('My Father, Shigeru Yoshida') by Kazuko Aso, Kobunsha, 1993.

Nobuaki Okubo (later Makino) aged 10 (left) and his elder
brother (seated), at the time they accompanied their father
Toshimichi Okubo abroad.

Countess Makino and her daughter Yuki.

Historical Setting: The Yoshidas in Grosvenor Square

By Ian Nish
Emeritus Professor of History, London School of Economics

Yukiko Yoshida published in 1938 a memoir of the two years she spent at the Japanese embassy in London, entitled *Whispering Leaves in Grosvenor Square*. The years 1936-8 were difficult years for Anglo-Japanese relations; but her memoir is non-political and scarcely contains any political comment. Instead, it is autobiographical and a commentary on the kind of diplomatic society in which she lived. It contains some of her poems about life in London, though this is only a fraction of her overall output which covers her experiences in Italy and Japan as well.[1]

In March 1909, Yukiko Makino (1889-1941) had

married Yoshida Shigeru who had entered the Foreign Ministry in the intake of 1906 and was about to be posted to the London embassy at the age of 31. Yukiko was the eldest daughter of Count Makino Nobuaki (Shinken), the son of Okubo Toshimichi, the great statesman of Satsuma and Meiji Japan. Makino had had a varied career as a diplomat and had spent over three years in the 1880s at the London legation. While he had served as minister in Italy (1897-9) and Austria (1899-1905), Yukiko had attended English-speaking schools and become highly proficient in the English language and literature. She had lived in a western environment during her formative teenage years. Shortly after her marriage, her father served as foreign minister in 1911-12 and 1916-18.[2]

Before Yukiko accompanied her husband as ambassador in 1936, she had three spells in London. In the first of these, the Yoshidas spent less than a year there in 1909-10 before departing for her beloved Rome. Then they stayed at the London embassy from 1920 for two years. The highpoint of these years was the visit to Britain in May 1921 of the Crown Prince (later to be the Showa Emperor). It was the first visit of its kind by such a senior member of the Japanese Imperial family as the heir to the throne and was a matter of great political sensitivity. Yoshida as first secretary had the responsibility to go to Gibraltar in order to receive the Prince on his arrival from Japan by cruiser. He and his wife had a prominent role to play during the visit and found it a moving experience.[3]

Next, Yukiko spent almost eight years in China

before her husband returned to Japan as vice-minister for foreign affairs (1928-30). The Yoshidas then went to Italy to Shigeru's first ambassadorial post. There Yukiko had the task of bringing up her large family of two sons and two daughters (one having died prematurely in 1915) while her husband was spending much of his time attending sessions of the League of Nations dealing with the Manchurian crisis.[4]

It appears that Yukiko accompanied her husband in October 1934 when he made an extensive tour as inspector-general of overseas legations. Travelling via Manchuria and Siberia, it took them to Europe and the United States, including a sojourn in London. Colonel (later Major-General) Francis Piggott writes in his memoirs of holding a party in London on 17 November 1934 at which Yoshida as 'ambassador-at-large' was present with his wife.[5]

RETURN TO GROSVENOR SQUARE

The background to Yoshida's appointment as ambassador to London, which might be described as the summit of the family's ambitions, was not a happy one. It was an indirect result of the plot to assassinate key political leaders during the Incident of 26 February 1936. Among those targeted for attack was Count Makino, formerly the Lord Keeper of the Privy Seal and therefore a close adviser to the Showa Emperor. Insofar as the army officers involved believed that the Emperor was being misled by his civilian advisers, they were gunning for Yukiko's father especially. Fortunately, he escaped from the inn where he was staying in

Yugawara by the rear entrance, with the help of his grand-daughter, Kazuko. This left the attackers so furious that they set the building on fire. The mutiny was crushed following an outright rejection of the cause by the Emperor who called on loyal troops to suppress it. It nonetheless caused the collapse of the cabinet. The genro's invitation to form a new cabinet was accepted by Hirota, in the formation of whose government Yoshida Shigeru played a large part. It was widely speculated in the press that Yoshida would become a member of the new ministry, probably in the role of foreign minister. But the army announced that he (among others) would be unacceptable. Perhaps the fact that Yoshida was the son-in-law of Makino may have contributed to his unpopularity with the army. In embarrassment, Hirota eventually decided to send Yoshida as ambassador to London after earlier rumours had evaporated. The Yoshidas departed for London on 21 May via Ottawa and Washington.[6]

The Yoshidas found themselves in a complex situation when they arrived in Britain. Britain had her hands full with the European crises of the day: Abyssinia and Spain. The Italians had attacked Abyssinia on 3 October 1935 and 50 nations had agreed to apply sanctions against them. Meanwhile, faced with the outbreak of civil war in Spain, the Baldwin cabinet (June 1935 to May 1937) decided on a policy of non-intervention. Britain was equally faltering in her approach to Japan, still expanding in China. Officials and ministers in Whitehall and outsiders differed among themselves in their prescriptions for the

most desirable course for Britain to take on the Far
Eastern scene. The Foreign Office was inclined to be
sympathetic to China and distrustful of Japan. Others
felt that Britain's limited resources should be concen-
trated on Europe, while she sought some sort of
accommodation with Japan.

Soon after the Yoshidas arrived at Waterloo Station
on 25 June, Yoshida wrote to his father-in-law that he
found the atmosphere on his arrival to be more friendly
than he had expected.[7] Mme Yoshida was, she writes,
delighted with London but the embassy located at 10
Grosvenor Square which had been left unoccupied
since Ambassador Matsudaira left in 1935 'was a
disappointment to us as it was so neglected, having
been vacant for ten months. We had to spend over a
month among cleaners and painters before the house
was habitable, and even now we are gradually
improving it when our Government allows us the
expense'. Moreover, everyone was out of town and so
the family set off to Scotland to stay with Catholic
friends, the MacEwens, at Marchmont House, Duns.[8]

The Yoshidas must have drawn some satisfaction
from the views contained in *The Times*' editorial of 8
August:

> A renewal in some form of the Anglo-Japanese Alliance
> would be a development welcome to Japan. It is true that
> Japan is very far from being inherently pro-British. Granted
> the expediency, however, there is nothing in the temper of
> the country to prevent an Anglo-Japanese rapprochement;
> and there is much in the traditions of both parties to
> forward . . . . [There are serious though not insuperable
> obstacles], nevertheless *this country would welcome the friend-*

Shigeru and Yuki with their first child Sakura.

Count Makino and family with Shigeru Yoshida and family at the Makino residence, Tokyo, 30 November 1929. Back row (L/R): Nobumichi Makino, Kenichi Yoshida, Shigeru Yoshida. Middle row: Yuki Yoshida, Sakura Yoshida, Count Makino, Nobukazu Makino, Masao Yoshida (standing), Mrs Nobumichi Makino, Countess Makino. Front row: Kazuko Yoshida (L) with Sadako, Michiko, and Yoshiko Makino. *Photo: Courtesy Nobukazu Makino.*

ship of Japan, a proud and gallant young nation for whom we have always had respect.[9] (My italics)

Whether this cordial reaction was the result of initiatives by the new ambassador is impossible to tell.

By the time the Yoshidas arrived in London, Japan's negotiations for an agreement with Germany had reached their final stages. Under the Hirota cabinet it was decided to carry on these talks during the summer, the Foreign Ministry taking over the negotiations from the army general staff. Yoshida certainly knew of the imminent conclusion of an agreement because General Oshima, the military attache in Berlin, came over to London to try on behalf of the Japanese army to convince him to support the pact. But he failed. The German–Japanese anti-comintern pact with its accompanying documents was signed on 25 November and published shortly after.[10]

Yukiko must have been aware of her husband's disappointment. The pact seemed to undercut what he saw as the aim of his mission in London, the need to win back British opinion for Japan. Yoshida embarked on the first phase of his overtures to Britain through the Conservative party in October on his own initiative and they continued in dilatory fashion well into the new year. He was careful to say that they were personal. Yoshida did not clear his actions in advance with Tokyo, probably because he knew that he was *persona non grata* with the military and, therefore, wanted to go as far as possible on his own. There were more hopeful signs when a ministry favourable to his approaches took office in Tokyo in January.[11] It seemed a good omen also when Neville Chamberlain with whom Yoshida and his wife had good relations took over as prime minister in May 1937.

It is clear from *Whispering Leaves* that the Yoshidas were devoting much energy to cultivating influential members of British society. They seem to have travelled most weekends, either to political country-house parties or for independent sightseeing. Sometimes Mme Yoshida went her own way and made her own contacts. Her interests were literary and she wrote a good deal of poetry in Japanese about London. She seems to have had an especially cordial relationship with Mrs Neville Chamberlain who had a high reputation as a charming hostess who took great pains over the welfare of ambassadors and their wives. Two of Yukiko's *tanka* are dedicated to Mrs Chamberlain.[12]

The ambassador and his wife were witnesses to the distress felt by the British people over the abdication crisis. In December Mme Yoshida who described herself as being a 'prisoner of the sick room' wrote: 'On the morning of 11 December I heard the sad news of the Abdication. . . I listened with emotion to the King's last speech on the radio which moved me greatly.'[13] She was not unmindful of the fact that Japan was also a monarchy and that Edward VIII as Prince of Wales had visited Japan in 1922.

The agony of the winter abdication was dispelled by the anticipation of a summer coronation. Japan had been determined to show herself on the international stage on a major royal occasion, the coronation of the British monarch. She had announced as early as

October 1936 that Prince Chichibu who had received part of his education in Britain would represent the Japanese Emperor at the ceremony. It was hoped that the visit of himself and his wife would have the effect of improving Anglo-Japanese relations. In due course, the Asahi newspaper sent coronation greetings for the coronation of King George VI and Queen Elizabeth by air on the Japanese plane named *Kamikaze*, built by Mitsubishi, which landed at Croydon airport after a record-breaking flight from Tokyo to London. The Yoshidas had to go to Croydon on 9 April in order to greet the crew-members, Messrs Iinuma and Tsuka-goshi, after their gruelling 94-hour flight.

Prince and Princess Chichibu travelled via Canada and arrived at Waterloo station on 13 April. They stayed at Hove for a month but came to London to preside at the Emperor's birthday (*tenchosetsu*) reception on 29 April. At a special banquet on that day the Yoshidas were the hosts for the Duke and Duchess of Kent, Prime Minister Baldwin, Foreign Secretary Eden and 5-6 cabinet members.[14] On the coronation day of King George VI celebrated at Westminster Abbey on 12 May, Prince and Princess Chichibu, representatives of one of the world's oldest monarchies, were given precedence over the other foreign royalties. These events were followed outside London by the Coronation Naval Review at Spithead near Portsmouth in which the Imperial Japanese Navy ship *Ashigara* took part.

The Yoshidas organized an elaborate royal dinner on 24 June in order to say farewell to the Chichibus but the Princess suffered from the first of a series of illnesses which delayed their departure for a tour of Europe. While they visited Switzerland and the Netherlands together, illness prevented the Princess from joining her husband on a visit to Germany.[15] They returned to London again before leaving finally from Southampton on 18 September via Canada.

This had been a taxing time for the Yoshidas. There had been a succession of glittering celebrations which had been the high point of Mme Yoshida's years in London. Understandably, however, the Yoshidas were exhausted and from 1 July they rented a country cottage called Little Fishery at Maidenhead for two months.

Mme Yoshida's health was always delicate and took a turn for the worse in August. Suddenly, she had to be taken from Maidenhead to the London Clinic and operated on for hernia. Yoshida wrote specially to his father-in-law on 23 August:

> Exhausted after the coronation, we rented a house at Maidenhead and we all moved there at the end of July. I am commuting back and forward to London for work morning and night and we are all comfortably settled. On the morning of the 20th Yukiko suddenly contracted stomach pains and we immediately called a doctor who diagnosed hernia (*kanton*). . . . You need not be unduly worried – it is not a major operation. After examination by a surgeon she was sent straightaway to a hospital called the London Clinic and had the operation as quickly as one might expect. There were no particular aftereffects and she is progressing smoothly. Today there is no pain any more; and she slept very comfortably last night.[16]

Around this time fighting broke out between China

and Japan. It initially seemed to be a small-scale event. But the undeclared war quickly escalated when the Japanese army in China intruded into Shanghai and the Yangtse valley. One of the people that Mme Yoshida had met was Sir Hughe Knatchbull-Hugessen, the new ambassador to China. But no sooner had he arrived there than his car was strafed by Japanese planes on his way from Nanjing to Shanghai. It was inevitable that many disputes between Britain and Japan would arise and many complaints would be registered. In some organs of the British press a sustained campaign in favour of China resulted. Left-wing demonstrations outside the ambassador's residence, threatening the boycott of Japanese goods, were reported from 24 September. Mme Yoshida was understanding enough to observe that 'British feeling naturally went with the Chinese' and in the months that followed 'noted the difference of atmosphere of the public towards us though our personal friends did not change'.[17]

LITERARY PURSUITS

During the long period of Yukiko's convalescence, she had to rely on her daughter Kazuko, now 23 years of age, to act as hostess at embassy functions. Thus, Kazuko was to address the Japan Society on 26 May 1938 on the subject of the 'Japanese Woman' – a subject which had not previously featured in the programmes of the Society. Some extracts may indicate her views:

> I undertook [this speech] only because I wanted to feel that, before leaving England, I had tried to do my bit for the

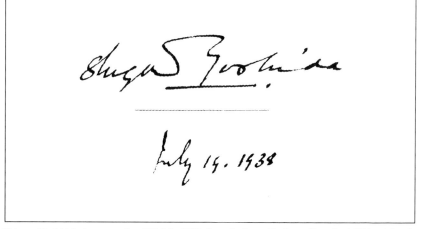

Shigeru Yoshida's signature, dated 19 July 1938, from the Japan Society of London's Visitor's Book.

cause so dear to my father's heart – that of better friendship and understanding between our two countries. . . . What I should like to introduce to you today is [not the geisha but] the average Japanese woman you or I would meet in Japan, her history, her education, her ideals and her failings. . .

In a busy day's round of golfing, riding or speed-boat racing a girl may return home to a quiet hour of tea-ceremony. In some cases this has no effect; but mostly it soothes and gives her back her equilibrium and her real sense of values. . .

In Japan, as most people know, it is a case of an arranged marriage. . . In the last few years there have been many more love matches like those all over the world, but whether these have a happier average is difficult to say. Parents usually have a wiser eye for the young; and, unmoved, or rather undazzled, by a Grecian profile or ravishing figure, their judgments are shrewder, especially where the future of a son or a daughter is at stake. A Japanese *mariage de convenance* is not the political or business alliance which a century ago existed the world over, for it only has for its object the happiness of the young couple. To those unused to such an idea it will seem incredible in this present age, but the answer is that to a Japanese the foundation of marriage is duty first, and then love.

. . . To the women who see in their past history only meaningless oppression and humiliation the modernisation of Japan has meant their rebirth or resurrection. Many feel that it is now the time to get their own back on their husbands. They join in the world chorus for self-expression, self-assertion, women's votes etc. . . We have learnt and gained much from our English sisters. Their frank open-heartedness, broad-mindedness and unfailing sense of humour have enriched our lives, but, I would like to add, there is beauty too in the delicacy and gentle strength of the women of Japan.[18]

We may imagine that in this speech Kazuko was reflecting some of the views of her mother.

It was during these difficult months that Yukiko's memoir, *Whispering Leaves in Grosvenor Square* was published by Longmans Green and Co. It carried a preface by Sir Francis Lindley, an old family friend, who had been ambassador to Japan (1931-4) and had since his retirement become chairman of the Japan Society of London.[19] It effectively closes at the end of 1937 and omits the events of 1938. It gives a straightforward account of the social contacts which the Yoshidas had made It presents a picture of the cordial atmosphere they experienced in the circles in which they moved and suggests that Yukiko was an active ambassador's wife. This picture is slightly at odds with that which memoirs on the British side have presented and which the Foreign Office records show. But it is historically important, nonetheless.

The memoir prays for peace in the war with China and implies that the Yoshida household at least was not in favour of Tokyo's policies. Yukiko's political thinking is not clearly expressed but it would appear from *Whispering Leaves* that she followed the British press closely. Hence her worries when her friend, Mrs Fleming, insisted on introducing her son, Peter Fleming, who had come out in the press with criticisms of Japan's actions in China and Manchuria in his capacity as travel-writer and reporter to *The* (London) *Times*.[20]

But *Whispering Leaves* was primarily a memoir of Britain written with the eye of an artist by a person of high culture. Yoshida's biographer in his critique of the work suggests that it exhibited to British readers the *yasashii kokoro* of Japanese womanhood.[21] That is, the kind-hearted, good-natured and genteel qualities of Japanese ladies. It shows that Yukiko moved not only in diplomatic circles but also in literary and artistic circles. She had meetings with Arthur Waley, Alfred Noyes and Leo Myers. The book also contains examples of her delicate *tanka*, traditional Japanese poems which she evidently wrote first in Japanese and then translated into English. They appear to have been composed as mementos for close friends or as personal reflections of English scenery.

BACK TO JAPAN

In August 1938 Mme Yoshida left London with her daughter for Japan. She had to arrange the wedding of Kazuko to Aso Takakichi which was due to take place in November. Yoshida himself returned to Japan on 19 October. The Yoshidas reached Tokyo at a time of anti-British demonstrations, organized by the army. While Hankow and Canton had fallen to Japan, the Chinese had shown no willingness to sue for peace and it was assumed that Britain was encouraging their resistance. It was even suggested that English language teaching should be given up in schools.[22]

London was the Yoshidas' last diplomatic post; Shigeru had reached 60, the age of retirement, and left Foreign Ministry service in March 1939. Despite this, they made a point of remaining in touch with Ambassador Sir Robert Craigie at the British embassy as also with Ambassador Joseph Grew of the United States. Craigie wrote of Yoshida in his memoirs – and one can reasonably associate his wife's name with this tribute:

> Yoshida never deviated from outspoken opposition to the army's whole policy of aggression abroad and oppression at home... While other friends fell by the wayside, Mr Yoshida never relaxed his efforts to avert the threatening catastrophe. He came openly to see me at the Embassy at times when I myself considered it unwise for him to do so. His ambassadorship in London was only one episode in a career devoted consistently and courageously to the improvement of Japan's relations with Great Britain and the United States.[23]

In the late summer months of 1941 when frenzied negotiations were taking place to prevent Japan's war with China spreading to a global war, Yukiko was taken to hospital. Shigeru was at the time busy making unofficial contacts around the Tokyo Club. Yukiko in her struggle to survive at a time when medical supplies were short because of the war emergency was helped by foreign friends. Eventually, she died of cancer of the larynx (*kotogan*) on 7 October at the age of 53. Her funeral was held under Catholic rites three days later.

As a devout Catholic believer like her daughter, the late Mrs Kazuko Aso, she was buried at Aoyama cemetery with a tombstone bearing the sign of the cross. The front of the stone is inscribed in the calligraphy of her husband: 'the grave of Yukiko Yoshida, Magdalena Sophia'. Adjacent to it were later placed the tombs of her father who died in 1949 and her husband.[24]

Yoshida Shigeru survived until 1967, becoming prime minister from 1947 to 1954, one of the longest stints of any postwar prime minister. His role in restoring Japan to her place in the international community doubtless owed something to the groundwork which he and Yukiko had done in Grosvenor Square.

The Yoshidas differed widely in tastes and character. Yukiko shone in things at which Shigeru was not good. She was interested in culture: she was gifted in oil painting and design and talented in languages. She had a benign spiritual quality: she was otherworldly and is sometimes described as an 'above the clouds person'. On the other hand, it is alleged that she was not a good cook or interested in housekeeping. She was more westernized than her husband, though he, too, was an internationalist, if in a different way.

Whispering Leaves shows that 1936-8 were difficult years for Anglo-Japanese relations and unhappy years for the Yoshidas personally. But the affection for Britain which Yukiko personally felt from previous postings in London stayed with them in these disheartening times and shines through its uncomplaining pages.

NOTES

1. Yuki Yoshida, *Whispering Leaves in Grosvenor Square, 1936-7*, London: Longmans, Green and Co., 1938. There are important articles by Terunuma Kobun, Kurihara Ken and Iokibe Makoto in *Ningen Yoshida Shigeru*, Tokyo: Chuo Koron, 1991.

2. There are references to Mme Yoshida in London in Inoki Masamichi, *Hyoden Yoshida Shigeru*, 4 vols., Tokyo: Yomiuri, 1981, vol.III, pp.7-111 [Hereafter cited as 'Inoki'].

I have published some studies of the Yoshidas in London, including 'Yoshida Shigeru and Mme Yoshida at the London Embassy' in *Britain and Japan: Biographical Portraits*, vol. 2, Folkestone: Japan Library, 1997, pp. 233-44; 'Ambassador at Large: Yoshida and his Mission to Britain, 1932-7' in Sue Henny and J.P. Lehmann (eds.), *Themes and Theories in Modern Japanese History*, London: Athlone, 1988, pp.195-212; and 'Mr Yoshida at the London Embassy, 1936-8' in Japan Society of London, *Bulletin*, 4(1979), pp. 3-7.

3.   F.S.G.Piggott, *Broken Thread*, Aldershot, 1950, p. 337; Nish, 'Crown Prince Hirohito in Britain, May 1921' in *Biographical Portraits*, vol. 2, pp. 209-10

4.   Ian Nish, *Japan's Struggle with Internationalism*, London: KPI, 1993, p. 49

5.   Inoki, vol. II, pp. 270-1; Piggott, p. 246

6.   Yoshida Shigeru, *Memoirs*, London: Heinemann, 1962, p. 13-14; *Kaiso 10-nen*, 4 vols, Tokyo, 1957, vol.I. Also John Dower, *Empire and Aftermath*, Cambridge, Mass.,1979, ch. 5; and *Japan in War and Peace: Selected Essays*, Cambridge, 1995, pp. 217-18; Ben-ami Shillony, *Revolt in Japan*, Princeton, 1973, p. 132

7.   Yoshida to Makino, 7 Aug. 1936 in Inoki, vol.III, p.29

8.   *Whispering Leaves*, pp. 10-11

9.   [London] *Times*, 8 Aug. 1936

10.   Yoshida, *Memoirs*, p. 15; Inoki, vol. III, pp. 17-20 quoting Tatsumi

11.   Yoshida to Makino, May 1937, in Inoki, vol. III, p. 45

12.   *Whispering Leaves*, pp. 40 and 50

13.   *Whispering Leaves*, p. 28

14.   Inoki, vol. III, p. 40

15.   Princess Chichibu, *The Silver Drum: A Japanese Imperial Memoir*, Folkestone: Global Oriental, 1996, pp.129-37; *Whispering Leaves*, p. 55; Inoki, vol. III, pp. 166-7

16.   Yoshida to Makino, 23 Aug. 1937 in Inoki, vol. III, p. 77

17.   Arthur Clegg, *Aid China, 1937-49: A Memoir of a Forgotten Campaign*, Beijing, 1989, pp. 74, 81-2. Inoki, vol. III, pp.64-5

18.   Kazuko Yoshida, 'The Japanese Woman' in Japan Society of London, *Transactions and Proceedings*, XXXV (1937-8), pp. 87-94

19.   Ian Nish, '"Jousting with Authority": The Tokyo Embassy of Sir Francis Lindley, 1931-4' in Japan Society of London, *Bulletin*, 105 (1986), pp. 9-19

20. Peter Fleming, *One's Company and Other Writings*, London, 1934 and *News from Tartary*, London, 1936

21. Inoki, vol. III, p. 167

22. Dorothie Storry, *Second Country*, Ashford: Japan Library, 1986, p. 51; R.L. Craigie, *Behind the Japanese Mask*, London, 1946, pp. 76-8; John Morris, *Traveller from Tokyo*, London, 1946, ch. 22

23. Craigie, pp. 171-2

24. Essays by Terunuma and Kurihara in *Ningen Yoshida Shigeru*

Ambassador Yoshida, his wife Yuki and daughter Kazuko, on their arrival at Waterloo Station, 24 June 1936.

On the Thames at Maidenhead. Shigeru Yoshida in front with dog, and behind him, Madame Yoshida (L) and her cousin Baroness Ijuin.

Whispering Leaves in Grosvenor Square

By Yuki Yoshida

W̲e left the *Berengaria*, on which we had enjoyed five days' voyage among British and American passengers, and alighted at Southampton on British soil after so many years.

I came here for the first time when I was nineteen years old as a young attaché's wife, and I fell in love with England and her people, and have never recovered from it since. So I was overcome with pleasure just to be in England again, only I wished I had come as a private individual, to have and enjoy a carefree life among English people.

Many kind people were at Waterloo Station to welcome us. It was Alexandra day and all the people wore roses, which looked like cherry-blossoms. We drove straight to Grosvenor Square, which is a dignified square but our Embassy was a disappointment to us as it was so neglected, having been vacant for ten months. We had to spend over a month among cleaners and painters before the house was habitable, and even now we are gradually improving it whenever our Government allows us the expense.

I arranged a tiny governess's room on the second floor as my study, re-papering the walls with silver and hanging mauve satin curtains at my sole window, from which I could see the roofs with chimneys, so cordial in the sun and resigned in the rain. On rainy days all the windows look so quiet, and sometimes a thin smoke begins to rise from one chimney.

Mrs McEwen kindly invited me to come and stay a week-end with her at Marchmont, and though I knew I ought to stay and supervise the cleaning of the house I could not resist the call from beautiful Scotland of which I had been dreaming so long. So I set out by the express 'The Flying Scotsman' one Saturday morning. The luxurious compartment was decorated with four pictures of Scottish scenery and two mirrors. I sank into one of the soft seats and lost myself in a quiet solitary world. The rain began to fall like silk threads on the field dotted with white and yellow camomiles, and on the trees through which some red-tiled houses were peeping. As the train ran, the rain came pouring down, effacing all the scenery and effaced me too into slumber. York station woke me up with a jerk. A fat man in broad green check scurried clumsily past my window though his luggage was carried by a porter who followed him. A pale-faced young mother hurried along with an apple-cheeked baby in her arms. And so the train puffed off from the station. The rain poured on, and an attendant asked me if I wanted anything so I ordered a cup of coffee which was so tasteless that it did not rouse me at all. White stripes moved in the grey under my window, and it was very unexpectedly the border of a sea. Fortunately, the rain had almost stopped when the train came into the station of Berwick. The chauffeur Mrs McEwen kindly sent said something to me when I was examining the post cards in the stand at the station. The drive was long, but I did enjoy the scenery of the country. Marchmont House stood in the midst of a beautiful wood dignified by the age of two hundred years. The lady of the house looked exquisite in mauve chiffon with a set of jewellery of amethyst that evening. I pictured her in Elizabethan dress with a lace ruffle round her slender neck and a pear-shaped pearl dropped on her high white forehead.

The view from the bedroom window was my favourite one. A wide green road in the middle of a rich wood went straight through what seemed miles, and beyond the dark forest were seen some remote hills where I wondered if happiness lived. I roamed about in the beautiful woods which surrounded the house listening to the orchestra of the birds as I strolled under the new green foliage. Some trees had just adorned themselves with their jewels of buds which I could not refrain from feeling for they looked so clean and sweet.

Some notes of the birds in the woods were so clear that they might have dropped on the moss as tiny crystal balls. I sat down on the grass near a brooklet in a meadow in the bosom of a forest among the sheep, and listened to the murmur of the water which ran glittering in the sun. We played croquet one afternoon in the front garden, but I did not know what I was doing, being too fascinated by the carpet of daisy-studded lawn and with the fountain which sprinkled silver. I could never express my gratitude enough to my hostess who had given me such pleasure I ever longed to have.

Next week-end I happened to be alone taking lunch in the small dining-room in our home in Grosvenor Square. The sky was grey and I took my solitary meal with a bowlful of pink carnations and a footman staring at me. I can enjoy London grey sky more leisurely on such occasions.

The first few weeks in July were spent in exchanging calls with Ambassadresses and Ministers' wives. Our doyenne is a charming and sympathetic lady for whom I began to form a special liking.

One fine July morning I started for a drive to Hampshire, to the home of a dear friend of mine, Lady Lindley. It was a long drive, but I enjoyed the beautiful fields and woods on the way. I could fancy a dryad under the thick foliage of beechwood with faint sunflakes on her golden hair. My friend welcomed me into her drawing room with its atmosphere of old England. After a quiet, enjoyable lunch I was taken round her garden. A clear noiseless stream runs across her velvet lawn, which I love among my many English treasures. Finally we went to inspect her well-kept glasshouses, where she insisted on cutting her beautiful white roses and a bunch of sweet peas for me. Even after several hours our conversation could not end, but I had to leave as I had an appointment with our doyenne, at whose house I met the Prince of Monaco buttonholed with a red rosebud. I have been to more sumptuous houses with charming hostesses but my friend's atmosphere stayed with me for several days.

My first experience of seeing a polo match was given to me by Lady Fawcett at Roehampton Club. The sun glistened equally on the emerald lawn and on the beautiful horses ridden by gay coloured players. I was struck by the luxury of the game, and became a great admirer of it. When luxury combines with danger then does it convey the real feeling of luxury.

One afternoon we drove to the Chiltern Hills. We sat down on the slope of the hill. Under the mellow sun of autumn, the soft grass mixed with wild flowers shone when the breeze blew and shed their sweet scent. A little boy ran after a white butterfly as his golden curls bobbed, a scene I shall always remember. On our way home we passed many houses with their windows half hidden with masses of roses in bloom. I wished I could live in one of them.

On the 2nd of July Her Majesty Queen Mary received us in audience at Buckingham Palace. The Queen, dressed in black with some white trimming and many rows of magnificent pearls about her neck, was standing in her drawing-room when we entered. It

was in 1921 that I curtsied in front of the same Queen
on her throne at a State Ball given in honour of King
Albert I of the Belgians. How deeply I admired the
stately and gracious queen then; her sweetness and
charm touched me deeply. The same thought came
back to me at this audience as she kindly took us to her
Oriental room, where she kept some Japanese and
Chinese curios in a cabinet. On taking my leave I
dropped a deep curtsy, from which I could not have
recovered unless the kind Queen had held me by my
hand.

The next morning greeted me with a blue sky and a
white cloud floating on a shining plane tree in the
square; each leaf of the tree shone with gladness,
adoring the sun. I could also see some summer-clothed
young girls walking blithely on the pavement, each
carrying a tennis racquet. I went out to Hyde Park after
breakfast and took a quiet walk in Nature's company.
The birds, dogs, sheep, horses and even the rabbits
looked so happy too in such a country. The happy
scene at any rate, consoled me. It was a sweet picture
that a mother duck made on the lake, followed about
by newly hatched ducklings, looking like floating
woollen balls.

A wooden box awaited me on my table when I
came home. On opening it a big Japanese doll
appeared, holding a playing ball between her long
sleeves, patterned with peonies. The whole of her
crepe-de-chine dress was covered with white and
mauve peonies, and a scarlet brocade 'obi' was tied at
her back. Her silky black hair and dreamy black eyes

made me feel homesick just for a few minutes. It had been sent to me by a friend of mine who had dressed it herself.

On the 22nd of July there was the Royal Garden Party at Buckingham Palace, and King Edward VIII was to receive five hundred debutantes besides the Diplomatic Corps and the dignitaries of the nation. The procession of gaily dressed young ladies seemed endless. In the tent a Court official approached and said something to the King, then His Majesty said in an undertone 'Oh some new Japanese are they?' or something to that effect and kindly gave us his hand and said a few words to us. I felt so grateful as I noticed how tired he already looked after receiving countless people.

A few days later Mr Wickham Steed, whom my father used to know in Vienna at the time of the Russo-Japanese war, came to have tea with us. His face is so aristocratic and his smile so gentle. I went to hear his lecture at the Friends' Hall later on; I would never have thought that he could look so stern or so heated.

It was in the beginning of August that we gave a luncheon party to Sir Hughe Knatchbull-Hugesson, who was then starting for China as British Ambassador. It was one of our early parties, and we had not yet time to recover our old drawing-room chairs, but the party went off cordially in spite of them. I never dreamt then what an unfortunate incident was in store.

Mid-August found us starting for Scotland. It was a nice feeling to leave the imposing stone house behind in a car with some trunks, which looked so carefree.

We ran through fields after fields, all shining under the midsummer sun. The scenery changed markedly after we crossed the border for Scotland. The heather-covered rocky hills replaced the flat fields, and herds of sheep grazed quietly on the slopes of the hills. I wished I could stop the car to come out and touch the sheep. We stayed at Taymouth Castle Hotel. From my bedroom window I could see a widespread emerald lawn and dark woods in the distance. The air and the verdure were purifying for my soul and body. The lofty drawing-rooms and especially the carved wood-panelled library made one think of the old glory, and of the people who should have been there. A spinning wheel with a carved horse head stood in a corner of the hall, and made me picture a vision of a maiden with long braids of golden hair hanging down from her shoulders as she deftly spins with her slender fingers.

We drove out to many different places. I love the key-note of Scotch scenery, rocky hills covered with purple heather, silver streams winding silently through and sheep quietly standing here and there. The black mountains awed me and I felt I could not breathe while we were passing between those deadly hills. We once met a mountain fog. It came so suddenly, rolling down from the mountain, gulping the woods, the road on which we were running, and even our car itself. I thought it even made a sizzling noise at is advanced, but as we stood there in deadlock for a few minutes, it began to clear, showing the ferns, sheep and a waterfall which I had not noticed before, and we could continue our journey in the scenery which could have been

washed by rain. My husband thought we ought to try
our hand at fishing as we were in Scotland, and hired a
gillie to teach us. The first fish we caught was a small
trout with tiny red spots. It looked too pretty to keep,
so I put it back into the river, and my husband teased
me, saying I should join the Committee of the
R.S.P.C.A. We drove across the Forth Bridge. I never
saw such a ferry boat before, which could take in over
twenty cars on board with passengers inside them and
on the deck. The bench in front of us was occupied by
a young married couple in tweeds, and a sweet white-
haired man with a green-eyed girl in a yellow coat.
The boat left the shore while a mongrel wagged his tail
to the girl, and a crying baby was heard from below.

On the morning we were leaving, the rain overnight
had enhanced the green world around Taymouth
Castle and made it still more green. On our way home
we stayed at the old town of York in a hotel which
used to be a convent. A castle in the distance looked
like a drawing framed in the foliage of oak trees which
stood in the hotel garden. We also stayed at the quaint
old town of Windermere and I wished I could come
back there again.

We returned to London to attend the Japan Society
dinner for the first time. I heard afterwards that about
three hundred and fifty people were present. At the
head of the banquet hall the huge flags of the two
nations were hung side by side. I had the honour of
sitting between our Chairman, Sir Francis Lindley and
Lord Cromer. One incident I remember so well was
that in connection with some conversation in which I

(L/R) Top: The Yoshidas leaving for tea at Buckingham Palace, 11 March 1937. The Yoshidas on Bournemouth beach. Above (L/R): Madame Yoshida and daughter Kazuko at Bournemouth. Madame Yoshida and Kazuko in Court dress leaving for the Presentation Ball.

used the phrase 'as Japan is poor', to which Lord Cromer replied, 'That is because you spend too much on your excursions in North China.' I only took it half jokingly at the time, as it could not be foreseen that our National Treasury would have to meet the burden of a war with China.

Towards the end of October I began to notice the leaves of the trees in the square turning yellow, and day by day they began to fall. One late afternoon when I looked out of my bedroom window, the setting sun was gliding on to the fallen leaves, and an old man rising from a bench walked slowly away, followed by a faithful dog. One morning I went into the square and sat down to rest.

IN GROSVENOR SQUARE

Sora sumité
Kogané ni konoha
Chiru asa o
Ukikoto wasuré
Odayakani oran.

Translation:

Under the limpid sky of morn,
Softly the golden leaves fall,
Alone I would be,
To forget the tearful world
And for a while be one
With this tranquillity.

We have to be very compact in making Japanese poems as we can only have thirty-one syllables in them.

I love the autumn leaves here, yellow is more consoling to me than our own scarlet leaves. When I walk under the tunnel of golden trees my heart gradually warms up.

I found a parcel from Japan on my table one afternoon, when I came in from a luncheon party. Opening it I found some silk and some sweets from my parents. I felt the happiness of having both one's parents still quite well and not too old. I thought of having a dress made out of the silk and spending a quiet day in it, eating the sweets they had sent.

We gave a luncheon party in honour of Mr Mackenzie King as he had so kindly entertained us at dinner at Laurier House in Ottawa. An Austrian violinist who had played at the Austrian Legation some nights before gave a recital after lunch.

We started for Brighton by car one morning. The fog made the roads wet and as there was hardly any traffic I could hear the faint hissing of the wheels of our own car. Some hills we passed were hidden halfway by fog, looking as if they had huge cotton wool caps on, and at their feet a few sheep stood with their coats almost dripping. We arrived at Princes Hotel just in time for lunch. When I sank down in an armchair in front of the fire I could just see from the window the tops of red buses and the seagulls passing to and fro. Two women who sat opposite talked on and on and made me feel drowsy. There was also an old couple on the sofa who did not utter a word for quite an hour; they must have kept their faith in each other all those years.

Next Sunday we drove out to Hindhead. The sky was clear blue and I felt the mellow sun penetrating through my back while I walked through a brown field with a few poppies left here and there. After taking lunch at a hotel there, my daughter and I sat on the lawn basking in the sun and looking at the autumn leaves. The surroundings were so still that I began to think the world belonged to us two, when a clear note from a bird in a tree near by startled me. On our way home I saw a pale gold moon rising above a now discoloured forest.

On the 3rd of November King Edward VIII opened Parliament. The day coincided with our great Emperor Meiji's birthday which we still keep as a day of celebration. My husband and I had the honour of attending the ceremony at the Palace of Westminster. It was an impressive scene with all the peers and peeresses and the dignitaries of the nation in full dress listening motionless to the King's speech. The King read his paper so distinctly that even I could understand every word.

We chose Torquay for our following weekend. There was no one else in the compartment of the train so we three monopolized it. The smoky houses and chimneys gradually faded away until at last a meadow dotted with cows appeared and some patches of shining water through the bare trees. In the back yard of a house a group of hens and sparrows perched together on a haystack, and some pigs grazed on the

grass, all bathed in the same mellow sun. I did enjoy
the scenery on both sides as our train ran towards our
destination. It must have been warmer at Torquay as
the hills there were still covered with golden leaves
and a patch of grey sea was seen between them. The
scene reminded me of Nara only we have no calm
shining sea there. I heard the young voices of golfers
who seemed to be oblivious of the scenery. We went
for a walk in the afternoon. As my husband and my
daughter went off exploring, I sat on a bench on the
cliff. The sea was one sheet of pearl grey which
disappeared into the sky, leaving no horizon, and even
the lapping of the sea on the shore did not break the
silence. Seagulls passed occasionally and vanished into
the sky. I was roused from my dream by a beautiful
golden cocker spaniel which suddenly appeared in
front of me and wagged his tail. A fashion parade and a
show dance took place after dinner as it was some kind
of a gala night that evening. We went upstairs and read
in our sitting-room before going to bed. The
armchairs were very comfortable under the soft light
of a stand. We spent only three, but ideal, days there as
we had to come back to London where my husband
had work to do.

We were invited by the Foreign Secretary, Mr.
Anthony Eden and Mrs. Eden to dinner about this time
at the Savoy Hotel. The present Prime Minister, Mr.
Chamberlain, then the Chancellor of the Exchequer,
and his wife were also there. Though I had had the
pleasure of seeing Mr. Eden before, it was surprising to
find a Foreign Secretary so young and I thought he

must have a brilliant brain to hold such a responsible position. Mr. Eden was so cordial to me during dinner. We were talking about certain articles in *The Times* and I also commented on the leader entitled, 'Three's Company' which had appeared a few days before. He said he would always remain a friend of Japan. I did wish in my heart that nothing disagreeable would arise between our two nations. I found Mr. Chamberlain so understanding, which is an important characteristic of great men. I remember talking to him about the birds in the parks, which made Mr. Chamberlain tell me that he went to St. James's Park in the morning whenever he had time, to watch the different kinds of birds that sojourned there. It reminded me of the book of Viscount Grey's letters to President Wilson exchanging views on the songs of birds, and how my father admired the sentiment of it and told some young Japanese to hold these great statesmen's spacious minds as their example. Mr. Chamberlain asked me if we really were afraid of Bolshevism. In answer I told him about my cousin, a young peer and his family, being kept in Russia, and though he is employed by the Soviet government as a stage superintendent it will not be easy for him and his family to come out of Russia. Another episode I remember during our conversation; we were talking about the origin of names, and when I said, 'Your ancestors must have been in the Court' he said, 'But innkeepers used to be called chamberlain too' and he insisted on that. I saw Mrs. Chamberlain for the first time and was struck by her gentle charm. I thought her face looked like that of a 'Kwan Non', goddess of

Mercy in Buddhism. I had no opportunity to talk to Mrs. Eden but I appreciated so much her handsomeness and youthful freshness. The evening will be remembered all my life.

When I looked out casually one morning I found that a grey uncompromising square building had suddenly sprung up opposite my bedroom window. All the leaves which had screened it had gone, leaving the skeleton trees. One tree arrested my attention.

FROM MY WINDOW

> Zokuyoku o
> Hitoha hitoha ni
> Nugisuté té
> Eda omoshiroku
> Tateru hadakagi

Translation:

> Shedding one by one
> Its leaves of worldly desires
> Like an old man the wintry tree stands
> With its branches picturesque and bare.

The busy social days continued. As I came in to change one evening a full moon was rising calmly and gloriously above the bare trees in the square. The scene cooled my whirling brain. But a little later when I passed Piccadilly Circus on my way to the theatre to see the play 'Storm in a Teacup', the electric signs ruffled it again, reminding me of the busy day I had spent.

We drove to Sussex one afternoon. The deep blue sky was broken with some floating white clouds, and a few tiny red berries were shining under the bare bushes. The winter trees looked as if they had begun to dream of spring seeing the blue sky again after so many months. While my other companions walked I sat on the grass, and drank in the air and the beauty of the scene. The huge red sun sank into the bare forest, and a few birds flying towards the golden sky looked so black.

I found my father's letter on my desk when I came home. I opened it carefully and read it over and over forgetful of time. As I still held the letter in my hand lost in my thoughts I could see my father through all the distance, in his favourite armchair writing this letter. When I ate grapes that night at dessert, the sweet juice made me think of him again.

To my great personal disappointment, I found myself a prisoner in the sick-room for much longer than I expected, and I was still ill in bed when the news reached me of the difficulty concerning the British Throne. I felt so sad about it all, as I realized to the full the terrible unhappiness that must be felt by the entire British Commonwealth. My thoughts were tormented as I lay in bed, as I sympathized so deeply with the distress overshadowing the nation. On the morning of the 11th December I heard the sad news of the Abdication. The fog closed in the windows of my room and only the subdued noise of the traffic reached me through the gloom. I listened with emotion to the King's last speech on the radio, which moved me greatly.

I heard the cannon celebrating the accession of the new king next morning. The grave events, handled so quietly and wisely did not even cause a ripple through the nation. Mr. Baldwin deserved the praise given him but this unblemished outcome of a difficult problem was the testimonial of the solidity of this great nation.

My old school friend in Tokyo asked me of my daily life and I wrote her a series of poems something like this. 'I am awakened in the darkness every morning by the sound of the hoofs of horses drawing little carts laden with fresh vegetables from the country being taken to the markets. There are different kinds of sounds of hoofs, some blithe, some heavy. I go to sleep again, and when I get up the morning is advanced. I clean my teeth looking at the bare trees in the square against the grey or blue sky. My bath wakes me thoroughly. The bubbling of coffee welcomes me when I come down to the breakfast room. It is a pleasure to pour out coffee from a silver pot into the indigo porcelain cup. My otherwise enjoyable meal was always perturbed by the articles in *The Times*. Sometimes I go out shopping. The shop girls are tidily dressed with nicely arranged hair and what I like about them is they do not pay unnecessary compliments, yet they never lack politeness or kindness. We often have some guests to lunch. The table is always artistically arranged by our dear friend Mrs. Edwards in good time. In the afternoon I go out to receptions, which pursuit I do not care for very much, but I make the acquaintance of many interesting people at these parties.'

I wrote as an example of one of the early dinners we were asked to, that of the Polish Embassy. Countess Raczynska made a charming and efficient hostess. The table was decorated beautifully with candles and delicate coloured flowers. I sat between the host and Mr. Duff Cooper, who toward the end of a charming dinner began to talk about 'the tales of Genji' and kept his conversation to literary subjects, which I also preferred to other topics. I did feel honoured to talk about literature with the author of *Talleyrand*. Lady Diana reminded me of the ladies if Grecian days. When I come home I usually take a cup of Japanese tea and then go to bed about twelve or later.

When I saw Mrs. Chamberlain at Mr. Eden's dinner she asked me if I knew any other of the Cabinet Ministers' wives and when I answered in the negative as I was only just beginning to go out, she so kindly said she would introduce them to me, inviting us together for tea. I felt her kindness so much. She asked me to lunch instead of tea. I was so excited to go actually to 11 Downing Street, as I had heard of the address and seen it printed all my married life. I loved the place with the atmosphere of history which no wealth can buy. I do admire the State Secretary's official residence, so unostentatious yet dignified, the dignity attained by tradition. It is in one of my favourite parts of London, Whitehall, with the tranquil park in front. The gentle and gracious atmosphere the hostess created blended so well with the intangible beauty of Turner's paintings which decorated the drawing-rooms of quiet taste. We were taking coffee standing after lunch, when one of the guests dropped her spoon, and I saw that more than one lady tried to pick it up for her. Then the hostess made an excuse for her guest, saying the spoon was too big for the saucer, but as they are rather expensive things she had not bought suitable ones yet. The simplicity and unpretentiousness of the English upper classes are so very pleasant. That scene will stay in my memory always and I shall treasure it with other precious memories I experienced among English people.

We began to have the well-known London fog to which many people object. But I think the fog is the veil of an artist, making the stately stone buildings look even romantic, and when the streets are lit the fog transforms the scene into a fairy city. And in the country it shades off woods and lakes like some black and white Japanese paintings. When the sun sinks into the bare wintry trees a mist makes the scene of the afterglow so remote yet pregnant with thoughts.

We went to Bournemouth to spend a few days at the end of the year. Branksome Tower Hotel is isolated from the town and is built on the cliff above the sea, so I could have both the scenery and the air to my heart's content. The hotel was so full that we could only have our rooms on the ground floor. But through the lace curtains I could see a few white camellias in bloom. The mixed notes of birds woke me up next morning instead of the noise of the traffic. The sapphire blue sky through the pine trees looked so unreal after London grey skies and more pleasant than real sapphire. On the beach, children and dogs ran happily together on the sand where the shining blue sea lapped. As the afternoon advanced, the sky turned pearl grey but it was beautiful to see the veiled red sun sink into the white sea with seagulls flying dreamily. At night a full moon hung low, blurred by mist and the dimly lit sea between the pine trees.

On New Year's Day the majority of the Japanese community in London came to the Embassy to pay their respects to our Emperor's picture, which was hung at the place of honour with purple (a colour much used at our Court) curtains, hung and divided in the middle, in a festoon shape showing the portraits of our Emperor and Empress. It must sound strange to English people to make a deep bow to a picture, but worshipping the Emperor and his family is a religion with us and we regard our Emperor as a sort of demi-god, for the founder of the Imperial dynasty was an Empress whom we believe to be the sun goddess, and whose descendants have been reigning over our country for nearly twenty-six hundred years.

We drank the toast of 'Long Life' to our Emperor with saké, our wine. After that the party relaxed and took refreshments, merrymaking. When all the guests dwindled away and only the Embassy staff and their wives were left we decided to play our national card game, which is an universal game with all classes in Japan and is called Hyakuninshu, which means 'A poem each from a hundred people.' There are a hundred cards, each bearing the lower part of a different poem by well known poets and poetesses of olden times. The players are divided into two parties and sit in a row facing each other. Fifty cards are given to each side and they place the allotted cards open in front of them. There is another packet of a hundred cards with the full poem written on each, and these are given to a reader who begins to read each poem on the card aloud, one after the other. The players look for the card with the right lower part of the poem, from the cards which are placed in front of them and their opponents and the skill lies in recognizing from the first words how the poem ends. If you take a card from your opponents' side before they do, you can give them one of yours so as to decrease the number of your own, and vice versa. Whichever side has taken all the cards first wins the battle. Before all the western sports came in, this game of cards used to be more popular, for it could be played so intensely and vehemently that it could almost replace a game of sport.

Madame Gripenberg called on me for the first time on 26th February. She was afterwards to become one of my most dear and precious friends. She struck me as a very unusual person and had an unworldly air about her which one values so much in people.

One Sunday morning I was doing my hair two fat sparrows came and watched me at my window, twittering to each other. I felt warmed by their company. I cheerfully dressed and went to church across the square where I go every Sunday. My little soul could drink in the pure morning air and the clear songs of the birds in the trees as I walked home.

We drove out to Tunbridge Wells. The sky was so blue that morning that even the little red brick houses in the outskirts of London looked smiling in the sun. Each leaf of the hedge in front of a house was shining and also the little red cheeks of a baby that lay in a perambulator near by. There was a deserted road with bare trees further on, and each little pool which dotted the avenue reflected the blue of the sky. We lunched at Calverley Hotel. A little roller canary was singing cheerfully in a cage which was hung in the bright corridor facing the garden, but somehow I felt unhappy for him. We passed a bleak village where two women one in black and the other in a brown coat, apparently a mother and daughter, were walking a Sealyham. They looked as if they would spend the rest of their lives there. The sun was just setting, gilding the pearl coloured water of the Thames when we passed Battersea Bridge.

We invited the Secretary of State for Foreign Affairs and Mrs. Eden to dinner about this time. We wished so much to express our warm feeling of welcome to them, and so I designed three dresses for some stage dancing for after dinner entertainment. The first dance was 'The Moonlight Sonata' for which I selected a plain silver lamé, and had it made into a dress of simple lines with a long flared skirt and long sleeves very wide at the end. Soft blue georgette, fifteen yards square provided an ethereal floating cloud enveloping the

Top: Ambassador Yoshida fishing for trout on the river Tay with Madame Yoshida sitting on the bank. Above (L/R): The Yoshidas stretching their legs on the drive to Scotland. Madame Yoshida among the Scottish heather.

dancer quite in sympathy with the mood of the dance which interpreted the sentiment of the music so faithfully. A diamond tiara was put on the dancer's forehead, and her silver dress dazzled through the cloud-like blue veil as she slowly danced impersonating the moon. The title of the second one was 'The Phantom'. A ragged soot-coloured dress was practically made by myself with many pieces of darker and lighter shades of grey georgette sewn on to the low necked bodice and to the short and irregular lengthened skirt. A few touches of gold were buried among the grey which shimmered now and again as she moved her supple limbs. I told the dancer to have the nails of her fingers and the toes of her bare feet varnished scarlet and her dark hair loose to enhance the gruesomeness of the dance and to make it more fascinating.

The third one was called 'The Lily' for which I chose a white crepe-de-chine dress of Grecian style with a border of silver braid. The thought of the dance was conveyed very gracefully by the dancer who held a living lily in her hand. I wished that my effort could amuse our guests.

I also arranged some flowers in Japanese style for our honoured guests. I found some pussy willow branches which I bent and arranged in a half-moon shape and some cream rose buds at the bottom of the branches in a bronze vase. We call the tallest branch in the middle 'Heaven'. The side one and the next in height is called 'earth', and the flowers at the bottom which we always put are named 'man'. The whole shape must be a half-moon, and the numbers of branches and also the flowers of countable size must invariably be uneven in number. In Japan we put the flowers arranged in this style on the recess in front of a picture scroll. But as we have no recess here I placed it at the side of a marble head of Venus and they created an artistic atmosphere together, the Venus and the half-moon.

The following week-end we went to Brighton. The sea was grey and calm and only the wings of the seagulls lost in the lapping waves on the shore could be seen white. The small apple trees in the hotel garden already had tiny red sprouts which must have unwound by the breath of the sea. We drove out to Rottingdean. The winter sun through the fine mist laid a faint golden veil everywhere on fields, shrubs, and on the brooks. As we drove on the mist lifted, showing a blue shining lake with bare trees whose branches glistened in the sun, telling the approach of spring. On our way home the huge golden sun was setting in a grove of bare trees, melting the fine twigs. Later on a crescent moon began to shine in the clear indigo sky, with a brilliant star hung beneath as if it might have been a drop split from the moon.

Monday morning greeted me with my father's letter which is more to me than a precious gift. My father sometimes writes to me in English as he spent his childhood in America. He is a great admirer of England and English people, so I became his disciple even as a child. He went to America with his father Marquis Okubo in 1870 when he was nine years old to be at the College of New Jersey with his elder brother, and came here when he was a little over twenty as a young secretary of our Legation as it was then and stayed several years. Together with Prince Iwakura my grandfather went to Europe and America to negotiate and establish the first trade treaty with foreign nations. For nearly three centuries Japan had retained its isolation, evolving a history and tradition all its own. The sudden opening of its doors to foreign nations and the revolutionary changes which followed were resented by the followers of the old school. But despite overwhelming difficulties the modernization of Japan was accomplished and before his assassination in 1877, my grandfather had formed the first Liberal Government in Japan. He had given his life to open his country in the true sense to give a new life to Japan, the life which has made our nation develop as it has to-day. When I left Japan to come here for the first time my father said to me, 'London is like some precious pearls, wrapped in silk and stored away in a bag, as you cannot perceive its glory all at once, but the longer you stay there the more you will be able to appreciate it.' What he told me was true, for I have learnt to cherish England more and more each day.

One fine afternoon we went to Bray to have tea at the Hotel de Paris. The weeping willows on the banks of the river were already brushed with light green, and the pink almond blossoms could be seen on the other side of the water through the faint green strands of the willows. The fine twigs of bare trees shimmered under the blue sky and the shrill notes of birds seemed to urge the spring.

We asked Mr. and Mrs. Chamberlain to lunch one day in March. We wanted to do our best to entertain them and as a part-expression of our wish I made a little Japanese poem for them. I wrote it on a square of gold paper with a writing brush and put it at Mrs. Chamberlain's place on the table:

> Haru tsuguru
> Urara no hikagé
> Sashi ireba
> Kamé no Sakura no
> Emité mukouru

Translation:

> When the serene sun rays,
> Foretelling the spring, come in,
> The cherry blossoms in the vase welcome
>   them,
> Smilingly unfolding their petals.

(Foretelling the spring meant Mr. Chamberlain's future position as the Prime Minister, and the cherry blossoms represent the members of the Embassy.)

That night I was taken ill. I found a pot of cyclamen at my pillow side next morning. In my fever I thought they looked like red fickle butterflies trying to fly off in all directions. The cloudless spring sky came into my window every day with the sun vainly inviting me to come out. Veronica sent me some irises which made me so happy. Some white and pink tulips reminded me of baby Michael from whom they came. Gaily coloured hyacinths reminded me of our dolls' festival in Japan, red, violet and pink stalks of flowers standing primly in rows looking like brightly dressed Japanese dolls on the shelves. A basket of blue irises and lilies of the valley came from my husband. I could imagine a dwarf's stage of the forest scene from 'The Midsummer Night's Dream'. Some fairies danced round the bush of little bell-like white flowers, and Puck sat on the moss starred with tiny forget-me-nots hugging his knees. The faint mauve polyanthus represented the giver well, who has some fragrance of the ladies from 'Pillow Book'. Two beautiful bunches of double violets arrived, one from my dear Lady Chatfield, and the other from my friend Mrs. Lancelot Edwards.

> Makurabé ni
> Hana no kaori no
> Tadayoi té
> Tomo no omokagé
> Mata ukabi kuru.

Translation:

> Your gift of violets sweet my friend.
> At my bedside lie,
> Their fragrance drifts to my pillow
> Forming a vision of your face.

> Sora mo hi mo
> Kotori no koé mo

Tabané kité
Yamu makurabé ni
Maki kururu sumiré.

Translation:

Sweet violets, the gift of my friend,
As if in a bouquet bring
The sky, the sun, and the song of birds,
To transform my dreary sickroom
Into the land from whence they came.

We went to St. Ives for Easter. Tregenna Castle Hotel is quietly situated on a sort of peninsula. What I saw next morning from my window was the soft blue sky seen through the fine net of twigs with the sea which extended to the same coloured sky. The fine morning beckoned us for a walk. The silence of the azure sky was broken by the song of a bird, and the dandelions in the field below looked still sleepy with daydreams. Each blade of grass was shining in the sun and the dandelions may have been dreaming of butterflies. My husband and daughter went out in the afternoon, leaving me with a book. I was lost in it in the blissful quietness till the sun went down, the twilight deepened, and when I looked up two or three crows were passing over the bare trees to return to rest. At the end of five ideal days we reluctantly left St. Ives.

We started for North Wales again to continue the interrupted journey for my convalescence. We ran through cheerful roads in the midst of new greens with

the other cars which had also begun their travel in
search of spring. The meadows were sprinkled with
daisies, and I wondered if the horses and cows spared
those tiny star-like flowers. I saw a small village which
consisted of thatched roof stone cottages with sweet
green doors, all clustered together in the sun just like
children. We stopped at Stratford-on-Avon for lunch.
The hotel was a sixteenth century house situated near
the Shakespeare memorial.

> Fumi no yo o
> Tokoyo ni térasu
> Na wa aréshi
> Kono chisaki machi
> Isao tsumishi ka.

Translation:

> What hast thou done, thou modest little town,
> To have given birth to that magic name,
> Which shines over the world of literature
> Through all eternity.

We arrived at Bettws-y-Coed about six-thirty, and
stopped at Waterloo Hotel, where we stayed when we
came over to England for the first time twenty odd
years ago. The stream which runs in front of the hotel,
and the trees and the hills have remained exactly the
same through these years. They seemed to live in a
world of their own far away from this world of unrest.
The clear noise of the stream was clarified still more by

the pure notes of the birds, and the beeches in the valley adorned with young buds half hid the stream. We stayed two days at Bettws-y-Coed and moved to Anglesey. The hotel, our home for the next few nights, was situated in the wood facing the main land with the inlet of sea between. The scenery almost compensated for the accommodations of the hotel. The mainland clad in new greens, floated just like an island in the silver water, and the mauve mountains were seen in the distance. I could see the train vanish into the wood with the white smoke lingering behind. Gradually the twilight began to envelop the scenery leaving only the twittering of the birds clear. The mountains, the land, the sea and the meadows were forbiddingly silent in the gathering dusk, and when they were on the point of being swallowed up by darkness altogether. We drove to Llandudno next day. We stopped at Conway Castle to see the ruins and to think over the old glory of the castle. I could see a beautiful court lady in elaborate brocade dress leaning at the window looking across the sea to find a boat in full sail coming into the bay. And what would she have wished at night as she gazed at the high tided sea gilt by the full moon. The lunch at the Grand Hotel Llandudno was delightful with a long and sophisticated menu to choose from, after the days of more primitive food at the other hotels. We took it on the extension on to the glittering dazzling sea which gave the air of the south of France. It was a long drive back to Anglesey, but I enjoyed the scenery all the more. The sheep were everywhere with tiny lambs so white and sweet that I did wish I could take one home.

I never knew they wagged their tails when they fed on their mothers' milk, I thought only dogs wagged their tails when they were pleased. In a bosom of a dreamy green hill a line of smoke was rising peacefully from the chimney of a solitary house. We came back to our London home just in time to welcome Their Imperial Highnesses Prince and Princess Chichibu.

On 10th April our aeroplane 'Kamikaze' (Divine Wind) sent by the newspaper 'Asahi', bearing with her messages of congratulation for the Coronation of King George VI safely arrived. We went to Croydon to welcome it. When I first noticed it, it looked as small as a dove in the softly lit pearl grey sky. It made two circles over the aerodrome and came down smoothly, but I was so struck by the smallness and shabbiness of it compared with the other machines there. I was so happy to find the two young men so simple. Lord Sempill, who was the first to extend them a warm welcome, was the first teacher of the art of flying in Japan. He is a true friend of mine.

Kreisler came over to give his annual concert about this time and we went to hear him at the Albert Hall. I was overcome by the beauty of his performance, which stirs souls. He could give pleasure to those who are happy and consolation to those who are in need. He is more than a king. I met him again at Lady Cory's next day and he was just as I expected, so simple and child-like.

Their Imperial Highnesses Prince and Princess Chichibu arrived on 13the April. We drove down to Waterloo Station to meet them. The road-side trees dressed in new green smiling under the morning sun, looked as if they joined us in welcoming them. We were so happy to see that their highnesses arrived in such good spirits. They went to stay at the Princes Hotel at Hove for one month before the Coronation. Their rooms looked so bright and cheerful facing the sea.

Soon after, our Ambassador to Moscow, Mr. Shigemitsu, came for a visit to London, so we gave a dinner for the Soviet Ambassador and Madame Maisky and the Chinese Ambassador and Madame Quo Tai-chi. After dinner I remember telling the Chinese ambassador that I had lived seven and a half years in different places in China, and how I loved the vast scenery of inland China, consisting of an immense sheet of brown earth and sky, and when spring waves her wand the new greens come out all at once, intoxicating the air. Mr. Quo appreciated my taste and said, I must have a poetic mind. I found him so easy to talk to and Madame Quo so sincere.

April 29th being our Emperor's birthday we gave a dinner and a reception in celebration of the day. Their Imperial Highnesses Prince and Princess Chichibu presided at both the dinner and the reception. We asked the presence of Their Royal Highnesses the Duke and Duchess of Kent, and invitation which the Duke of Kent very graciously answered himself. We shall always keep his precious letter as our family treasure. Our dinner guests besides Their Royal Highnesses were the Prime Minister and Mrs. Baldwin, Mr. and Mrs. Anthony Eden, Mr. Malcolm Mac-

Donald and Mr. and Mrs. Walter Runciman, Lord and Lady Cromer and some others. The table looked rich with crimson and cream roses and the charming presence of the Duchess of Kent and our young princess enhanced its beauty. The stately dinner mellowed into a friendly atmosphere as the courses went on. Over seven hundred guests came to the reception which followed and all were received by Prince and Princess Chichibu. I can still picture the duchess of Kent in a beautifully cut white satin dress, and her broad diamond bandeau looked so proud to be adorning such a handsome head. It was after one o'clock when everyone left. I thought the party was a success and I did hope our guests enjoyed themselves.

As my husband had a cold I went to the Marchioness of Londonderry's reception alone. Just after I was received by the host and hostess I saw Mrs. Chamberlain standing and she so kindly suggested taking me round as her husband also was not there, attending a men's dinner. As it was just a short time before Mr. Chamberlain became the Prime Minister the guests greeted her all the more. Mrs. Chamberlain so kindly and patiently introduced me to each one saying, 'As we are both without our husbands to-night we are going round together.' 'I am taking her round,' a less gentle and cultivated person might have said. I admired her so much that I made some poems to express my feelings.

TO MRS. CHAMBERLAIN

Wakamé sashi
Momohana sakasu
Haru no hi ni
Tatoété taru ya
Kimi no onsaga?

Translation

To the beams of the sun
That in springtime
Full many a flower bring
Scattering its sweetness abroad
I shall liken the richness of thy heart.

TO MRS. CHAMBERLAIN

Chihiro no umi ni
Eteshi madama mo
Hikari nashi,
Kimi oba tomo ni
Eshi o omoéba!

Translation

A pearl of great price
From unfathom'd depth of ocean brought
Is naught when compared to the joy of my heart
Thy precious friendship doth impart.

The first Court was held on 5th May which coincided with our boys' festival day in Japan. On this day to wish prosperity to our boys' future we fly, attached to a high pole, huge carps sometimes as long as twelve feet, made of cotton or paper which streams in the air. A carp has special significance for our boys for it is called the 'samurai' among fishes. Against the strong currents and even up waterfalls they climb and yet when they are finally caught and placed on the kitchen board they do not wriggle but are calm and resigned. In our recess, the place of honour in a Japanese room, we place dolls impersonating different heroes, to wish for heroism in our sons. Some of these are centuries old and are veritable works of art. On 3rd of March we also have a dolls' festival for girls. We place the dolls of the Emperor and Empress in classical dresses, in front of a pair of gold screens on the highest of seven shelves, all covered with scarlet cloth. Then the Court ladies in white dresses and scarlet skirts come on the second shelf. Five musicians sit on the third shelf for they are supposed to be entertaining the Emperor and Empress. Next we place some historical ladies or people from fairy tales on the fourth and fifth shelves. Dolls' furniture in gold and black lacquer on the sixth and on the last shelf all the delicate food in miniature size served in tiny lacquer dishes. At night small paper lanterns are lit with candles which give a fairy-like air to the dolls. I read a fairy tale as a child of all the dolls coming down from their shelves and taking a bite from the dishes, laughing and talking, and when dawn began to break they flew back to their positions on the stand,

Ambassador Yoshida leading Their Highnesses Prince and Princess Chichibu at a garden party for the Japanese community at the Hurlingham Club, 23 May 1937.
Photo: Courtesy Diplomatic Records Office.

Japanese Embassy staff and their wives assembled at the residence before leaving for King George VI's First Court at Buckingham Palace, 5 May 1937. Madame Yoshida is in the centre; Kazuko is on her left with flowers. Ambassador Yoshida is eighth from left.
Photo: Courtesy Diplomatic Records Office.

motionless and mute once more. Some old-time people founded this festival to strengthen still more the bond which ties the nation to the Imperial family and also to make little girls interested in housekeeping from childhood. Some of these dolls are handed over from mother to daughter and in old families dolls of a few hundred years are still kept.

To return to the night of the Court, all our Embassy staff who were attending the Court, first assembled here, and we took a photograph together as a souvenir. My daughter looked like a fairy child though she is dark, and not quite ethereal enough, in a white tulle dress trimmed with yards and yards of thin white satin ribbon which made one think of water ringlets in moonlight.

The King was in naval uniform but his chest was so covered with orders that the ground cloth was hardly visible. The Queen was radiant in pure gold lamé with a blue ribbon across her shoulder. I shall cherish all my life the kind smile the Queen gave me when I curtsied in front of her. I felt as if I had become a middle-aged Cinderella lost in the splendour of the scene. The huge chandeliers, their light diffused through a thousand pieces of crystal, shone on the magnificent jewels and dresses and on the decorations and uniforms. It was such as pretty sight when the young Queen came down from the throne on the King's arm and made a curtsey to us before leaving for the supper room. The Polish Ambassador took me in to supper.

Mrs. Hill invited us to lunch one lovely day to see the cherry blossoms round her house in Kent. We started in the morning and as we left London entirely behind I saw a tunnel of young-leaved trees with dandelions scattered gold under it. I tried to see the scenes of fresh green which seemed to fly into our car windows, but my tired head was overcome by drowsiness. I was wide awake, however, from my stolen nap when we arrived at our destination. Our friend's house is a real British home, so simple yet dignified with the spirit of tradition so characteristically British and yet it corresponds to our old 'samurai' spirit. The cherries on the hills around look just like white clouds, and the sheep with lambs were standing about under the blossoms. The scene looked like an oil painting. The lambs were sweet in their white woolly coats, with their black eyes set wide apart under their little round foreheads. Mrs. Hill took me round her children's rooms after lunch. In one of them hung a picture of a child and a St. Bernard dog sitting together on the hearth rug. The child is trying to talk to the dog which hangs its head sadly. It is entitled 'Can't you Talk?' The sweetness of the picture made a lump in my throat. Mrs. Hill promised to ask me again when the trees will be laden with glistening ruby fruits.

Nature seemed to join in the preparation for the Coronation of King George VI and Queen Elizabeth. All the trees put on their new green garments, and the birds were singing their songs of felicitation. Even the humble dwellings in the remote suburbs were decorated with paper flags, sometimes evidently the work of eager children, not to mention the sumptuous decorations of the West-end houses and streets, in fact the whole of London. Apart from the warm feeling they expressed I must say all the decorations, even the best ones, spoilt the appearance and the dignity of London. London does not need decorations. With the sky also I prefer grey for London.

The traditional greyish morning greeted the long awaited 12th May. Getting up at an unearthly hour I dressed myself in silver lamé with a diamond tiara and three feathers in my hair. We left home at half past six, and yet the streets were already lined with people and the stands were almost filled. Finding our name cards quite near the throne we sat down reverently. As there were still three hours before the ceremony began I watched the peeresses pass in front of us in crimson robes with magnificent tiaras. Their robes are so aristocratic both in colour and style, which conform with the atmosphere the wearer creates. As the hour drew nearer the solemn music on the organ pulled me together.

Their Imperial Highnesses Prince and Princess Chichibu entered the Abbey through the west door, advancing slowly with composure and respect, leading the other foreign royalties. The solemnity of the moment was heightened by the anthem exquisitely sung by the choir when the King and the Queen entered from the west door, in stately procession. The ceremony had begun. It was so impressive when the people cried out 'God Save King George' in one loud unanimous voice in answer to the King when he faced the four different directions for his recognition. Then the King took the oath, answering either with 'I am

Prince and Princess Chichibu (top left), Westminster Abbey, for the Coronation of King George VI, 12 May 1937.

Madame Yoshida with Japanese air force pilot Masaki Iinuma at a celebration dinner held at the Savoy on 15 April 1937. The pilot (with mechanic Kenji Tsukagoshi) had flown the Mitsubishi plane *Kamikaze* (Divine Wind) to Croydon Airport, London, with a message of greetings, peace and cordiality to the British people. *Photo: Courtesy Japan Society.*

willing' or 'I solemnly promise so to do', in a low but earnest voice. As my seat was just behind the throne I could not see the details of the ceremony. But I was entranced by the feeling of solemnity and the beauty of the scene enhanced by the heavenly music.

I was once startled from my reverie by the dazzling splendour of His Majesty's gold robe, and I thought that all those rich embroideries round his robe must each signify something. After the great ceremony was auspiciously ended, and when their Majesties came down the steps of the theatre in front of us in their purple and ermine robes with the regalia in their hands, I was struck by the beauty of Their Majesties' faces, so ethereal and unselfish, that the sentiment of the vows they had just made to give themselves up for their people and country must still have been shining through. I felt that this noble couple were well suited to be the King and the Queen of this great realm, and at the same time, I thought of the richness they must feel to preside over this wonderful people and country.

Their Majesties gave the State Banquet next night. The young prince of Hesse took me in to dinner. The table was decorated with deeper and lighter shades of vermilion flowers filled in three vases of heavy gold which were placed alternately with the gold candle-sticks. In fact, everything on the table was gold. The King and the Queen looked so kind talking to our Prince and Princess, who sat next to them. The table was occupied by all the royalties and some ambassadors and their wives. Though I was overwhelmed by the honour, I enjoyed so much the gentle atmosphere which can only proceed from highly born people. That same atmosphere toned down the rich gold ornaments on the table.

We followed the royalties into the smaller drawing-room after dinner. The Queen, Queen Mary and all the British and foreign royalties in their dresses of lamé with their exquisite jewels looked like fairy queens. I tried to record the scene in my memory. We went to the receptions at the German Embassy and the Austrian Legation that same night.

We had the honour of attending the State Ball again the following evening, 14th May. In the magnificent ballroom, men and women in their full dresses dance together, looking like glittering whirlpools. It was so pretty to see the red-uniformed King and white-gowned Queen dance together.

One Sunday a few weeks later Mr. Malcolm MacDonald kindly invited us three to his country home in Essex. The house, situated in the middle of an open field, was originally a Tudor farmhouse re-done in excellent taste. There were just four of us at lunch in the quiet dining-room. The butler was dismissed after he served us the meat and our host poured some white wine and table water for us. I never was so impressed at any lunch as this one, being served by such a great person in the true sense of the word. After lunch Mr. MacDonald took us into his garden of lawn and dragging out some deck chairs asked us to sit down. The simplicity of nature which is common with great men is the most pleasant quality and is real dignity. I shall always treasure the memory of that day.

Among the many dinners and receptions of the Coronation year I remember that of the Marchioness of Londonderry's dinner, when our Prince and Princess Chichibu and the King of Egypt and the Queen Mother were present. Lady Londonderry looked so handsome, and she is a lady with personality. Her magnificent jewels dazzled me. I loved the long dining-room with marble statues in niches. From there we went on to the reception at the Duchess of Sutherland's. I sat at supper between the Marquis of Londonderry and the Duke of Westminster. The latter said to me, 'I hear you dined at the Londonderrys', then you must be hungry, you must eat more.' Then Lord Londonderry made some joking remark in retort. The huge ballroom was crowded with royalties, peers and peeresses and dignitaries, all in their full dress.

It was such a change to go down to Portsmouth on board the *Strathmore* and attend the coronation Naval Review. I could revel my eyes in the sceneries which came into our train windows. The different shades of green of the forests vied with each other under the mid-day sun of late spring. And in the meadows where the summer colts were rising, the cows were grazing sleepily. When we came aboard the *Strathmore* the evening sun was gilding a strip of the blue sea. I saw so many little boats pass loaded with people who were also going to see the review. A comfortable cabin was allotted to us as we had to stay overnight there. I remember sitting at the same table with Sir Robert and Lady Craigie and the American Ambassador and Mrs. Bingham. The day was a little misty, but we could see the Review beautifully. It was a grand sight. All the British warships and those of most of the other nations were of a grave grey. I do not like the purpose of warships but I do admire their appearance, so dignified and composed. Looking at all the magnificent men-of-war I could not help thinking if each country could keep the wealth spent on them, those nations could be richer enriching their people. We unfortunately could not stay for the illuminations at night and had to come back to London the same evening.

A garden party was given in honour of Their Highnesses Prince and Princess Chichibu at Hurlingham Club. About sixty Japanese children performed some athletic sports in front of their Highnesses. At the opening of the sports they formed huge British and Japanese flags by holding different coloured cloths, which was very cleverly and well done. Afterwards we all assembled on the lawn, gathering round the Prince and Princess and photographed together for a souvenir. As we still had a warm sun we got off at a meadow on our way home. The soft green grass was sprinkled with daisies and young-leaved beeches spread their boughs above. A roof of lapis lazuli and a floor of agate would fade away in front of nature's beauty.

Mrs. Ronald Greville gave a dinner in honour of the King of Egypt and for our Prince and Princess. There were over forty people present. The pleasant string band was playing in one of the parquet floored drawing-rooms, but no one danced. The guests sat round in groups and chatted comfortably.

The Caledonian Ball given on 28th May was a grand

spectacle. I felt so sorry that our Prince and Princess could not come owing to their colds as they would have enjoyed it so much. The floor of the vast hall was of polished ivory coloured wood which gave a clean yet mellow appearance to the hall. The little boy bagpipers were sweet, all of them looking so proud of their performance. I was told that the pipers had taken such pains to learn the Japanese anthem for Their Highnesses. However, I only realized the tune after it was too late! But I felt the cordiality of our hosts very much. The men were in kilts and the ladies also wore sashes of different tartans, which made the scene very decorative. The Scotch dances were very exciting with their occasional yells. It was a remarkable entertainment altogether.

We picnicked in a wood near Henley one day. After the chaotic lunch the others left for a walk and I lay on the fallen leaves in the wood. The blue sky could be seen luminous between the young foliage and the occasional sharp notes of birds startled me. I could also see afar the glistening meadows sleeping under the young summer sun. We took tea in a restaurant on the Thames. The gay parasoled boats, followed by the swans were passing the shining river, telling us that summer had really come.

On the 24th of June we gave a farewell dinner in honour of Prince and Princess Chichibu. The table was decorated with lotuses than in bloom, a flower at once elegant and remote. The guests were Mr. and Mrs. Neville Chamberlain, Mr. and Mrs. Anthony Eden, Viscount and Viscountess Hailsham, Sir Samuel and the

Lady Maude Hoare. Earl and Countess of Bessbor-
ough, Earl and Countess of Airlie, Marquis and
Marchioness of Londonderry, Mr. Hore Belisha and
Mr. Duff Cooper and Lady Diana Cooper, and some
others.

Lady Airlie who also gave us the pleasure of having
her as one of our guests will always live among my
treasured memories of England. She is just like a
portrait of an oil painting or of a more delicate
miniature of a French Court lady come out of a frame
with all the charms and the spirit of an English one. It
was such an opportunity for me to dine with these
people and I shall remember them all my life. Of one of
the guests I wrote:

TO VERONICA

Kofuno
Mimiwa zogeiro no
Kata ni yurasu
Kimi ni fusawashi
Veronica no mina.

Translation

Over thy shoulders
Of ivory colour
Waver the ear-rings
Of classical design.
Exquisite as thy name
Art thou, Veronica.

We dined at the Chinese Embassy the next evening. It was a Chinese dinner and my days in China came back to me. Our fellow guests were mostly American. Madame Quo Tai-chi looked particularly smart that evening in a close fitting dress of navy blue taffeta with thin white stripes, and with a magnificent diamond brooch to complete her smart appearance.

One night we dined at the Dowager Lady Swaythling's, who is a great friend of Japan. I was excited to see such great literary men as Alfred Noyes and Leo Myers, who were also there.

We took a little house on the river at Maidenhead for the summer, and moved there on the 1st of July. The Little Fishery was the name of the house which I loved. The little house was much better equipped than our Embassy in Grosvenor Square, having more spare bedrooms in a smaller space. We could see the shining river through the bright geraniums on our verandah, which scene reminded me of my friend's poem from Santiago saying that her young, happy days were reflected in the geraniums blooming in masses everywhere there.

I could hear the rustling of beech leaves when I often lunched alone in the quiet dining-room with the faint scent of roses coming in through the window. I loved to read in my study facing the river, and often when I looked up from my book I saw a black cobalt coloured bird hopping round the lawn.

The swans passed in front of our garden. One morning I took some bread and hopefully threw it to one. To my delight the swan deigned to stop and pick it up. Thus we made friends, and by and by they used to come from afar whenever I called to them. The ladylike swans looked so defenceless when the north wind made waves on the grey river. Whenever I saw them pass I used to run with a bag of bread. I came to know two mother swans with a group of young ones each. The mothers never took the bread, giving it all to the youngsters. One of the swans came alone one evening. I fed her, asking her where her mate was, and when I looked up from her I saw a full moon rising over the fir tree.

My quiet life was broken one morning by the news in the papers that fighting had begun between Japanese and Chinese soldiers near Peking, but no one knew then what large proportions it was to take.

On the 17th of July we went to Ascot. Their Majesties graciously invited the chiefs of the missions of the diplomatic corps to lunch and tea, and I had the honour of sitting next to the Duke of Gloucester at lunch, after which we came out to the stands. I saw the King whispering something to the Queen, who was following eagerly the approach of the horses. The jockeys perched on the heads of the saddles, and the eyes of the horses strained with excitement and their ears stood back as they flew cutting the wind. As they rushed up shining in the sun, carrying the gay coloured jockeys, the nose of the winner drew up by an inch. We had begun to withdraw ourselves when the Queen was beginning to say something to me about the horses. I always treasure the Queen's sweet smiles and her unselfish personality. The Duchess of Kent looked especially beautiful that day in a white dress with a big white empire hat, with a sapphire blue ribbon tied under her chin. She had ear-rings of diamond and sapphire in a modern setting which gave a finished air to her elegant appearance. If she had walked in a corn-flower field, she would have looked like young summer personified.

Prince and Princess Chichibu came to pass an afternoon on the river with us. I was so happy to find the Princess looking so well after her long illness. They admired the villas with beautiful gardens on both sides of the river and the Prince took some Ciné-Kodak pictures in colours which I afterwards heard came out very well.

I planned to go for a walking tour towards Henley by myself, but naturally when I saw a shaded field I stopped, and went on the soft grass to rest. The only objects which came into my eyes were the green grass and the trees shining as they waved in the breeze. As I sat there lost in the green world the rustling of leaves suddenly stopped, and a jet blackbird descended from a branch above me on to the grass, cutting the strong light. My cousin and his wife Isao came to stay with us for the summer. Isao reminded me of a gardenia, 'Kuchinashi' in Japanese, which means mute-flower, for she used to sit on the verandah making her baby's clothes day after day talking very little and looking like a white flower with a faint scent.

July 22nd was an eventful day, as there was a Royal garden party and also Mr. Myers very kindly asked me to lunch at Quaglino's to meet Arthur Waley. I was in great anticipation to see Mr. Waley as I am one of the fervent admirers of his work. He had a brownish check suit with a speckled red tie in a bow. He has a peculiar personality which is not awe-inspiring but has a strange force. He talked to me in the beginning but finding me insipid stopped and turned to his right-hand neighbour. I had heard that he had never been to Japan nor would come for fear of disillusionment.

Following this memorable luncheon I went on to attend the Royal Garden Party. The conflict in China had begun to take on a larger scale, and British feeling naturally went with the Chinese. We noted the difference of atmosphere of the public towards us, though our personal friends did not change. It was windy and clouded when we were standing among the crowds in the garden of Buckingham Palace. My miserable feeling was amply repaid by the kindly smile of Her Majesty which she gave me when I curtsied deeply to her. I was not feeling too bright either in the refreshment tent, when struggling her way through the crowd, the Duchess of Northumberland offered me a warm cup of tea and some sandwiches. I thought of the lady who looked like a magnificent statue standing at the back of the Queen on the throne at the time of the Coronation. I shall always treasure the spirit of 'noblesse oblige' of the English upper class.

The quiet life in beautiful Maidenhead relaxed me. I read Mr. Myers's *The Root and the Flower* in this suitable surrounding, and I was often lost in the beauty of the world the author created. Every scene of it comes back to me so vividly even now. I used to go on the river in our little boat. When it was fine the multi-coloured flowers in the gardens of the villas reflected themselves on the river as if weaving brocade into the water. As we moved smoothly, swans sometimes followed us and they always reminded me of fairy tales. The vivid green of the trees on the banks seemed to drop its emerald on the water and almost dyed the wings of the swans. In the morning when the river was smooth and mirror-like, a swan floated in the distance like a lotus flower just opened. And as the sun rose higher the river was troubled by passing boats, excursion boats laden with people, others more exclusive, and boats of all kinds splashed along the glittering river, but when sometimes the traffic suddenly ceased, the water reflected the sky and the trees just as before.

My breakfasts in my quiet dining-room were often darkened by the articles in the papers. One morning my vexed eyes were met with the new leaves of a fir tree, washed by the overnight rain, as I lifted them up from an unpleasant article. One does not mind criticisms if they are true, but I have been so unhappy for the one-sided comments which seem to drift Anglo-Japanese friendship further and further apart.

As I came down for breakfast on the 18th of August with the papers, I suddenly felt a pain in my side. I thought of taking an hour's rest before my painting teacher came, but I could hardly climb up the stairs to my bedroom. By the time the doctor came in the afternoon I was wondering how one could live through such pain. a surgeon arrived a few hours later to see me. They took me to the London Clinic at once,

Madame Yoshida feeding a swan at Maidenhead

and I was operated on at midnight. I enjoyed my ride in the car with my daughter who accompanied me for my pain had been dulled by an injection. When the doors of the operating theatre closed on her I wondered if this might be a real parting. In a small darkened room I tried to breathe in the anaesthetic as hard as I could for I did not like the idea of the operation being begun while I was still conscious. When I vaguely gained my senses I was lying in the middle of a darkened room with a nurse standing by. As I had been praying that I might offer up my life to restore peace in the East I was wondering if my prayers had been heard, but I soon realized that such an unworthy life as mine could not replace anything so important.

The first flowers I received were red carnations which I found next morning near my pillow. Mrs. Gwynne so kindly came to see me in the heat bringing sweet lavender bags which I still keep under my pillow. All the different kinds of flowers in blue, purple, white and red, with their different scents gradually filled my room, telling the different natures of those friends who had given them to me. Flowers being my favourite luxury, I did enjoy them so much. Little pink heads peeped through their light green calyxes which folded them lovingly, and opened day by day, finally proudly flowering into dauntless gladioli, which reminded me of the growth of a happy girl. My daughter came to see me every morning and stayed nearly the whole day. Though I knew she was coming I was impatient to see her whose company I enjoy best. She is my dearest friend. I watched over my children in the basic sense of right and wrong carefully until they were ten or twelve years old, suppressing my desire to fondle them but after that I have been educated by them in turn. I don't believe in the method of bringing up children telling them what to do in trivial matters and continuing to do so till they are almost grown up.

I revelled in the beautiful flowers my kind friends sent me, and I felt I must learn their charitable attitude to others, giving them pleasures each in their own way with their characteristic colouring and scent. My husband brought me carnations in sophisticated maroon, rust and cream. Four nurses attended me in turns. I can never forget their kindness. I thoroughly enjoyed my stay at the Clinic and felt reluctant to leave. My young nurse took me to my car which was standing at the entrance. I was so delighted to see the London streets again, and so happy to find myself still in them. I had to go back to Grosvenor Square as we had taken the house in Maidenhead for only two months. I often pictured those two swans waiting for me in front of the garden to be fed and the thought made me sad.

On the 18th of September, Prince and Princess Chichibu left England taking the boat from Portsmouth. We went to see them off. It was not nice seeing their white handkerchiefs, getting smaller and smaller as the boat went further away. I did fervently wish Their Imperial Highnesses a very pleasant journey.

We drove on to Bournemouth to stay for a few days. Towards dawn the next morning I dreamt a pleasant

dream while subconsciously listening to the songs of
the birds. We drove to Lulworth Cove after breakfast.
The leaves of the groves had begun to turn yellow, and
the dull light on them already told the loneliness of
autumn. And in the field overhung with the low sky a
flock of crows were flapping their wings against the
wind trying to take flight.

Madame Kurusu our Ambassadress in Brussels
invited me and my daughter to come for a visit so
we took an Imperial Airways plane from Croydon.
My daughter has always flown over to the Continent
and back but I had never had the opportunity before.
The machine began to traverse the field chasing the
crows, suddenly it left the ground leaving the houses
below. Though I flew surrounded by clouds, and then
above the clouds I could not feel I was elevated from
this world of trouble at all. The clouds gradually
cleared away after we crossed the Channel, and
Belgium lay stretched below us. All the ground was
cultivated into square farms like a map which
reminded me of Japan, only we have ranges and
ranges of mountains besides. Our Embassy in Brussels
was so daintily and comfortably furnished by Madame
Kurusu who lavished her kindness upon us during our
stay there. She took me to lunch at the Château
d'Ardenne next day. The soft autumn air prevailed in
the garden. The golden leaves of an old chestnut tree
reflected in the pond and a huge bronze horse which
stood up in the water looked warm, enveloped in
yellow leaves.

A little boy was born to my cousins, Baron and

Baroness Ijuin soon after our return to London. They had been staying with us at Maidenhead during the summer, and as the stars had been so beautiful there I suggested the name of Stella if the baby were a girl, and my daughter chose Michael if it were a boy. It happened to be a beautiful Michael that arrived.

One late summer morning, we started for Cambridge. The sun was so warm that we stopped the car and took a walk in a field where here and there a few tiny poppies were still left like unquenched hopes in the withered field. I held my breath when we entered Cambridge town, struck by its quiet dignity. We went to see King's College as my son had been there. The lofty stone gate mellowed with age, and half covered with ivy, and its wrought iron doors gave me a lasting impression. The historical chapel on the right made me feel reverential even though we did not enter it. What I valued most, was the cloister with the afternoon sun casting the shadows of the pillars on the stone floor of the corridor, and the square of velvet lawn in the middle. It would make the most flighty people pensive. The air conceived of tradition and philosophy must bring up men with deep thoughts. If a boy educated in such surroundings still remains otherwise, it is his own lookout.

The quiet scene of the square was so inviting when I came into my bedroom, one afternoon, to take off my hat, so replacing it again I stole into it. The greenness of the lawn looked more vivid where the trees cast their shadow, and the gold of the fallen leaves came out in relief. While I was day-dreaming the colours of the flowers in the flower bed became dim in twilight and a few more golden leaves fell noiselessly into it.

There was a State Banquet in honour of the King of the Belgians. The King was in a plain khaki military suit, looking so young. I was taken in to dinner by Herr von Ribbentrop. After dinner we were shown into a smaller drawing-room where the royalties and Ambassadresses were. I can never forget the incident when Queen Mary so graciously came to where I was standing and asked after Prince and Princess Chichibu. I felt the Queen so graciously sympathized with me in our present situation.

We had the honour of attending the State Ball the next night. It was so pretty to see the King in an evening suit and the Queen in a silver dress with panniers gliding on the reflecting floor and I could occasionally see a glimpse of the Queen's smiling face in the midst of the jewels and decorations.

Some crimson rosebuds which I arranged in a cut glass vase on my bookshelf welcomed me one morning with their coyly opened petals when I entered my dear little study. One of my friend's letters brought some snapshots of beautiful scenes in Surrey. A mist-covered lake embraced in the heart of a forest of bare trees is faintly coloured by the setting sun, I wished I could caress the little lake by putting my cheek on the surface of the rose-coloured water.

On the 9th of December I attended my first English wedding, that of Miss Mary Lindley. It was at her cousin Lord Eldon's place in Hampshire. It began to snow after we left home by car and I did enjoy driving through the beautiful snow-covered scenery. The bride was exquisite and her beauty made her look spiritual. She looked like the spirit of a lily in her lily-like white satin dress, and she scattered its scent when she smiled.

I did feel so much for dear Lady Lindley in parting with her daughter as I shall be in the same position soon. We consider the snow as a lucky omen in Japan saying it foretells a good harvest, which means prosperity and happiness to us agricultural people. So I wished with all my heart that our dear friend's marriage would be so.

I met Mrs. Valentine Fleming at a luncheon party. Though I talked with her all through lunch I did not know who she was, and only at the end of lunch she told me she did not see much of her son, who was busy writing for *The Times*. As I assiduously read that paper every morning I could not help asking who he was. I was surprised to hear that he was Peter Fleming. I had read so many of his articles which had sometimes vexed me, and I was curious to know him. Mrs. Fleming kindly asked me and my daughter to her fancy dress ball.

Mrs. Fleming's house is Turner's house. It is so quaint and mellow and I surmised the ballroom was the painter's studio. The hostess wore a vermilion crinoline dress with her hair of the same colour. It was so striking and she looked so young. There were so many interesting people in interesting dresses, among them the Austrian Minister whom I could not recognize until he gallantly came and greeted me for he looked so buoyant as if he had cast off many years. When I began to take leave Mrs. Fleming said, 'You must see Peter', and brought Mr. Peter Fleming to me in the corridor where I was standing. I talked with him for a little time. He looked such a sincere man and I am certain that he never writes anything unless he believes it, and the conviction changed my opinion towards him and ever since I have never felt angry even when he was rude to us in his articles.

I was in my study one evening looking at the flower-like snow falling quietly on the roofs in the mauve dusk, thinking it gently covered the roofs to send them to sleep, when someone knocked at my door, and handed me a parcel. It was a muslin bag full of rose petals and some other flowers of sweet scent so kindly sent by Lady Whyte. I liked it best among all my Christmas presents.

We went to Bournemouth again to spend the end of the year. On our way we stopped at Winchester to have lunch. At the bleak hotel I thought of Jane Austen who was born in so unromantic a place and yet made her name immortal.

Branksome Tower Hotel this time gave us a lovely suite of rooms on the top floor. The sea surrounded our sitting-room, and when we arrived, the sun was gilding the waves just under the pine trees and the rest of the sea was one blue which stretched to a sky of the same colour. When we drove in the afternoon next day my husband simply slept the whole way and back for the heavy burden on his shoulders must have been too much for him.

I saw a clear unbroken rainbow which stood like a

Kazuko Aso (1915-96) – memorial photograph.

huge luminous bridge and in the field under it some horses were standing shaking their tails. The evening brought us to a sweet village nestled at the foot of a hill and the smoke from the chimneys from cooking the simple evening meal shaded the bare trees behind. I tried to go to sleep that night listening to the sound of the waves but it only brought back to me the thought of the troubles in China.

Index